SCOTTISH WRITING
AND WRITERS

SCOTTISH WRITING
AND WRITERS

EDITED BY

NORMAN WILSON

THE RAMSAY HEAD PRESS · EDINBURGH

© 1977 The Ramsay Head Press

First published in 1977 by
The Ramsay Head Press
36 North Castle Street
Edinburgh EH2 3BN

ISBN 0 902859 40 4

Printed in Scotland by
Macdonald Printers (Edinburgh) Limited
Edgefield Road, Loanhead, Midlothian

Contents

ACKNOWLEDGEMENTS

Much appreciated help and advice was received in producing *Scottish Writing and Writers*, particularly in the compilation of the reference sections. The Editor is especially grateful to Dr W. R. Aitken, Miss Mary Baxter, Stewart Conn, Douglas Gifford, Trevor Royle and Frank Thompson.

The Scottish Accent

NORMAN WILSON

IT IS not altogether surprising that a nation which has become politically and economically absorbed in an incorporating union should find its cultural achievements, however distinctive they may have remained, generally regarded as part of the intellectual corpus of the larger country with which it has been integrated. So Scottish literature, with the exception of work in Gaelic, has come to be considered for most purposes as English literature.

Because of various problems of classification the practice is difficult to break, but it does throw up some strange anomalies. The *Oxford Book of English Verse*, for instance, includes poems by Barbour, Henryson and Dunbar who wrote in their native Scots when it was the language of the court as well as of the people and whose work has no connection with English literary traditions. In 1966, it is true, an *Oxford Book of Scottish Verse* was published, and though it was the intention of the compilers, John MacQueen and Tom Scott, to lay greater emphasis on verse written in Scots as opposed to English, it did help to gain wider acknowledgement of the quite independent character, quality and traditions of Scottish poetry, not only prior to the Union but up to the present day.

But though on a language basis it is easier to gain acceptance of the Scottishness of verse written in Lallans, the name sometimes arbitrarily given to Scots, there is no reason to think that a writer is any less Scottish when using the English language, which may be his normal, or indeed his only, medium of expression. His racial—or, if you will, genetic and ethnic—characteristics will reveal themselves, if only subconsciously. His cast of mind, his inherited attitudes, his phraseology, will in greater or lesser degree depending on the nature of the subject with which he is dealing, influence what he says and how he says it.

No one thinks of American writing as a part of English literature. In the two hundred years since their emancipation the Americans have evolved a style of English which has differences in idiom and syntax and is enriched with words and phrases drawn from the polyglot origins of the United States. It is as full of Americanisms as early Scottish-English writing was full of those Scotticisms which the eighteenth century *literati* were at such pains to eradicate in an attempt to conform to a mythical "British" culture.

By pursuing their own uninhibited way the Americans have produced, unselfconsciously, a vigorous prose style which is as expressive of the American ethos as Lewis Grassic Gibbon's linguistic experiments were of the Mearns in *A Scots Quair*, which he wrote with the lilt and rhythm of the Scots tongue, flavoured with a minimum but judicious use of native words for which there is no precise equivalent in English.

While Gibbon has been faulted by some critics for an over-indulgence in a kind of prose-poetry which sometimes appears a mere mannerism, there is little doubt that had he lived he would have moulded and developed his idiomatic style, which might, as he put it, have "a sense of something foreign" to English ears but would have been as understandable as the prose of a modern American novelist.

Even if writing in orthodox English the Scottish author cannot escape the compulsion of his genes, and his native instincts will inevitably assert themselves. A man who wears a worsted suit—or jeans and T-shirt—is no less a Scot than one who flaunts the kilt. David Hume, who strove to write impeccable English, was undeniably Scottish in his mental processes and philosophical attitudes.

Most Scots are still bi-lingual, using something approximating to standard English in formal communication but reverting to Scots in one of its many dialects, or to Gaelic, in conditions of intimacy or emotion. In a literary context, the cultured Scot, unless he has had an anglicised "status" education, usually has a fairly good knowledge of the vocabulary and literature of the vernacular, even if he seldom speaks it.

Hugh MacDiarmid, the inspiration and driving force of the Scottish Renaissance movement of the 'twenties and 'thirties, believed that Scotland could only recover its soul by going back to its true traditions and by revitalising the Scottish language as a literary medium in which the national genius could most effectively find expression. With an international reputation as one of the great poets of the modern world, he has had a tremendous influence on Scottish writing. Apart from re-animating the vernacular, in which most of his best work has been done, his great achievement has been in stimulating a whole generation of writers whose work reflects a flourishing of the Scottish spirit on a level of accomplishment which has rarely been equalled.

If the movement originated by MacDiarmid created a sometimes obsessive concern with being above all "Scottish," and some excesses of literary chauvinism, that was perhaps not unnatural in the early stages of regeneration. Even so, one of the most sensitive poets of the revival, the late William Soutar, sensed that behind the genuine impulses there lay "the dangerous seduction of taking refuge in the womb of the past and calling it rebirth." But though writing in Scots may have its limitations, in the sense that it means speaking to ourselves instead of to the English-speaking world at large, our life and our literature would be the poorer without the invigorating and enriching use of our native tongue, which is as vital a part of our inheritance as the blood in our veins.

When that fine Scottish critic, Edwin Muir, whose writing in English gained him a European reputation, once said: "No writer can write great English who is not born an English writer and in England," MacDiarmid's reply was "Back to Scots." But before MacDiarmid's impassioned plea John Buchan, in his introduction to *The Northern Muse* in 1924, was advocating the wider use of English with a "slight admixture" of Scots words and phraseology—a practice, of course, in which Burns himself had engaged.

"I can imagine," said Buchan, "a Scottish literature of both verse and prose based on this 'slight admixture,' a literature which should be, in Mr Gregory Smith's admirable phrase, 'a delicate colouring of standard English with Northern tints.' In such works the drawbacks of the pastiche would disappear; because of its Northern colouring it would provide the means of an expression of the racial temperament, and because it was also English, and one of the great world-speeches, no limits would be set to its range and appeal."

The point, which still seems necessary to emphasise, is that in whichever of our three languages the writer chooses to express himself what he has to say is ultimately what really matters.

If, after the long years of frustration which have inhibited and often thwarted the Scottish genius, we can break free from the trammels of national assertion and devote ourselves to individual creativeness we may begin to make a significant contribution to world literature. It must ultimately become stultifying to remain closeted "in a room with only one view from its single window," to quote a phrase used by Douglas Gifford in *Scottish Fiction since 1945*. This is not to say, of course, that we should betray or ignore our native traditions and inherited characteristics. The Scots are Scots, as indubitably as the English are English or Americans American. That is a fact of life, self-evident and inescapable;

9

and, hopefully, the need for affirming our national identity, necessary as this has been, may soon have lost its motivation.

The present volume is concerned with works written since the end of World War Two, a period which has seen both a resurgence of the Scottish spirit and a growing comprehension of the wider world beyond the horizon—a dichotomy of heart and mind consistent with the Scottish temperament which, for better or worse, has always been able to encompass the seemingly irreconcilable (the famous "Caledonian anti-syzygy").

In examining the nature of recent Scottish writing, the various traditions from which it has drawn nourishment, and the different directions in which it has moved, the survey reveals a remarkable diversity of talent and purpose, of achievement and experimentation. Not the least significant developments to which attention is directed are in broadcasting and the theatre. The challenge of working outside traditional literary disciplines has been eagerly accepted by a number of young writers and they have responded with a succession of talented and impressive contributions to radio and television which deserve a greater measure of critical appreciation than they receive. There is no doubt that this new vein of creative activity possesses exciting possibilities.

What the future holds for literature and the arts in general in Scotland depends on changes in the structure of society and on the new ideas and philosophical conceptions that evolve from such changes. But in whatever medium and in whatever way the writer chooses to illumine the Scottish scene, or any other scene, perhaps he is more likely to do so with integrity and a clearer perception if he remains uncompromisingly himself, conscious of his roots and all that has gone to make him what he is but unencumbered by ancient emblems and dogmas.

Scottish Fiction Since 1945

DOUGLAS GIFFORD

IT IS arguable that the Scottish novel is at once the most neglected and the greatest of Scottish literary forms. The force and variety of the Scottish tradition of poetry from Dunbar and Henryson to Burns and MacDiarmid, together with the critical failure in properly appreciating the really important achievements of the nineteenth century novelists, tended to obscure the fact that it is the novel form which has endured when Scottish poetry and drama either failed or bastardised themselves. Only recently is that mis-appreciation of Scottish fiction being set right, with the work of Scott, Hogg, Stevenson, MacDonald, Gibbon and Gunn being seen for what it really is: a school of Scottish fiction, with co-ordinates, governing ideas, symbolism and techniques which are distinctly different from those of other traditions. Scottish fiction has a function and a meaning the real power of which was sadly too often misunderstood and relegated to the edge of serious literary consideration. Modern Scottish fiction is still, in the main, very much in that tradition and still not seen clearly for what it is.

The nineteenth century Scottish novel fell into four types, all of which are very much with us. In ascending order of achievement, these were the "kailyard" and domestic novel, with its roots in bad Burns and Galt, and flourishing in Barrie and Crockett; the romantic historical novel, derived from Scott and maintained by writers like James Grant and Neil Munro, Crockett and John Buchan; the deeply serious satire on Scottish *mores* which has the bleakest of messages about Scotland, which goes back to Scott's *Waverley*, Galt's *Entail*, and was continued by Stevenson, Douglas Brown and John MacDougall Hay; and finally the attempt in fiction to envisage a whole Scotland, either of a Golden Age prehistoric period, or in a nostalgic lament for a way of life simpler and more profound and integrated than that of today.

The last two traditions or types are still the area of major achievement in Scottish fiction. The outstanding feature of that revival of Scottish fiction in the 'twenties and 'thirties seems to me to be the emphasis amongst the major writers on a perspective and value structure which transcends

and backdates the Scottish present and the recorded, historical Scottish past.
"It is a far cry to the golden age, to the blue smoke of the heather fire
and the scent of the primrose! Our river took a wrong turning some-
where. But we haven't forgotten the source . . ."
argued Neil Gunn in *Highland River* (1937); as did Lewis Grassic Gibbon
in *Sunset Song* (1932), Eric Linklater in *Magnus Merriman* (1934) and
many others of the period like Naomi Mitchison and "Fionn MacColla"
(Tom MacDonald)—and indeed the exploration of myth and the belief
that it offers a fundamental level of awareness more important than the
immediate awareness of the contemporary was basic not just to the
novelists of the period, but to the poets like MacDiarmid and Muir as
well.

Basically the shared idea was that the major events of Scottish history—
the organisation of the tribal peoples into property-owning and separate
hierarchies, the Reformation, the Highland Rebellions and Clearances,
the Industrial Revolution—were corrupting events, leading the Scot (and
the Scot as archetype for Western man)—away from his "golden age"
self, a self instinctive and primitive, but nevertheless sophisticated and
desirable. And although it seems clear that the supreme achievements of
the Scottish epic and mythic novel belong to the 'thirties, it no longer
appears valid to me to see the second world war as a dividing barrier as
it were between the first great creative wave of the "Scottish Renaissance"
and a post war subsidence of energy. If one looks at the novels of this
kind and their "spread" in time, it becomes clear that both the threat
and the fact of the war were issues which drove writers like Gibbon and
Gunn to their highest endeavours—producing work like *A Scots Quair*
(1932-34), *The Silver Darlings* (1941) and *The Green Isle of the Great Deep*
(1944); and producing, immediately after the war, but very much in the
same epic tradition some very fine individual novels—especially Fionn
MacColla's *And the Cock Crew* (1945); Naomi Mitchison's *The Bull
Calves* (1947); and Neil Paterson's *Behold Thy Daughter* (1950).

MacColla's novel, the most deeply serious of them all, is concerned
with the tragedy of the Highland Clearances. It is a starkly fatalistic
dramatisation of the conflict in the mind of a good, harsh and devout
Presbyterian minister, as he struggles to reconcile his feeling that the
Clearances are the punishment of God with his natural benevolence
towards his people. But it transcends this. For in the arguments with his
arch-foe, the poet Fearchar whom he has banished up the glen years
before, we are witnessing in symbolic form the archetypal Scottish debate
between the ancient "golden age" truths and the powerful distortions

with which history has bent and banished them. The theme, as with Gunn's *Butcher's Broom*, but set out without Gunn's redeeming optimism, is that of Paradise Lost, and it leaves a bitter taste in the mouth, like that barren nostalgia which David Craig deprecated in the ending of *A Scots Quair*.

There seems little doubt that this nostalgia and bitterness permeated the Scottish epic novel completely in the post-war years. Gunn's own fiction continued till 1954, with fine novels of the search for spiritual fulfilment like *The Well at the World's End* (1951) and *The Other Landscape* (1954). But apart from *The Drinking Well* (1946), he ceased to attempt that epic projection of his central characters on to the higher plane where, as with Finn in *The Silver Darlings* or Young Art and Old Hector, they represented a higher Scottish destiny and a rediscovery of vital roots. The later Gunn fiction is quieter, more introspective and less ambitiously "Scottish." And *The Bull Calves*, Naomi Mitchison's sweeping account of her Haldane ancestors of Gleneagles and beyond them the Scotland of the 1745 rebellion is haunted by its theme of a Scotland divided, the great theme of Scott and Gibbon of wholeness lost, but with a new sadness, an emptiness which was even more disappointing in the work of the most promising of the new writers after the war. Neil Paterson's *The China Run* (1948), and his grandly conceived study of a fishing community in the North-East, *Behold Thy Daughter* (1950) with its impressive central figure of Thirza Gair, the tough fisher-girl, suggested that here was a successor to Gunn and Gibbon. Indeed, Thirza seemed to have a satiric edge lacking in Chris Guthrie or Finn of *The Silver Darlings* but the promise that Thirza showed of emerging as a powerful symbol of Scotland's vital essence deteriorated into conventional melodrama. Paterson was to abandon the novel for fine work in the cinema, and one can only speculate as to where a career in fiction would have taken him.

The 'fifties in Scottish fiction were on the whole quiet years when established talents like those of MacCrone, Blake and Linklater continued the themes and attitudes of the 'thirties. New work tended to be satiric, as with Robin Jenkins, the major new writer of fiction to emerge. For the reappearance of what I feel to be the highest and finest endeavour in fiction, that attempt to celebrate and ennoble man's life in art, one has to wait till the 'sixties; when relatively suddenly a major group of Scottish novelists emerged, all of whose work was primarily concerned—albeit with all sorts of regional differences of subject matter and situation—with the traditional central issue of important Scottish fiction—that of dissociation of personality within a backward, narrow and intolerant

13

country, and the difficulty of discovering a whole identity which nevertheless had its roots in its own race and place.

To my mind the finest and most courageous of these new novelists is Alan Sharp. His *A Green Tree in Gedde* (1965), won the Scottish Arts Council £1000 prize for the best novel of the year. It was the first part of a proposed trilogy, of which as yet only volumes one and two, *The Wind Shifts* (1976), have so far appeared, Sharp having moved to Hollywood to write film-scripts (out of which an excellent novel on the American West, *The Hired Hand* (1971), has emerged). It seems unlikely that the trilogy will be finished; but *A Green Tree* can stand on its own. It tells of Moseby, a restless married student from Greenock, whose life, as we meet him, is about to change drastically (which is why the wind will shift for Moseby and friends in book two). But he is not the only major focus; the Cuffees, brother and sister, from Knutsford, are incestuous lovers whose lives also are breaking through pressures, while most important of all is Harry Gibbon (shades of *A Scots Quair*?), descendant of an old West of Scotland family, craggy individualists who sleep in the Greenock cemetery and whose lives are described in an early chapter of astonishing and succinct power. Gibbon, it emerges, is identified with the central symbolism, magnificently controlled, of *The Green Tree*; for as the meaning of the tree symbolism emerges, we discover a significance and power as deep as that of any of the Renaissance novelists and poets. One of Harry Gibbon's ancestors has been a country preacher—but not a ranting Puritan, rather a strange Earth-lover, a semi-pagan who took part in harvesting and seedtime, who lived life lustfully in the fullest sense, and who preached wholeness of response, wonder and delight. He—in his misunderstood surviving sermons and in his descendant, slow, lithe, wondering Harry Gibbon, haunts the contemporary situations of slum Glasgow, the beautifully evoked Clyde Littoral, London, Paris, the seedy digs and the pretentious parties. In short, Sharp attains a symbolism married with concrete control which rivals the Lawrence of *The Rainbow*, and certainly stands as the outstanding positive statement of modern Scottish fiction. Unfortunately *The Wind Shifts* is not so controlled, moving too swiftly as it does all over Europe, and changing its idiom unpredictably into Kafka-like strangeness of setting.

The Orcadian George Mackay Brown has achieved a much larger body of work. *A Calendar of Love* (1966), *A Time to Keep* (1968) (short stories), *Greenvoe* (1972), *Magnus* (1973), (novels), *Hawkfall* (1974) and *The Sun's Net* (1976) (short stories), are all the work of a literary craftsman with an informing vision. Brown too believes in completion and wholeness, and indeed the entire symbolism of his work is consistent, moving in a slow circle as it does round the Cathedral of St Magnus in Kirkwall—and not just moving in space, but in time also, since Brown sees the self-sacrifice of Earl Magnus in Egilsay as an Orkney Crucifixion, a re-enactment of Christ's redemption of fallen man as well as a murder described as though it took place in a modern concentration camp. Like his Orkney predecessor Edwin Muir, the fall of man is paramount in his work, and like Muir he is a poet whose work, poetry or prose, is characterised by a limpid simplicity which is deceptive, belying the deliberate and sometimes consummate artistry beneath the surface. But it seems to me—and I freely admit here that such comparisons are odious—that compared with Sharp, or, say Crichton Smith, he is *too* fixed in a *prescriptive* vision. His Catholicism—a strange Orkney hybrid of pagan celebration and reaction to the bleakness of the Reformation—compels him to a predictable denouement, and increasingly in the later work—as with the explicit miracle that ends *Magnus*—an artless obviousness and repetitiveness of situation and image. Tentatively I suggest that his case is the sad one of a truly great writer who has chosen to live in a room with only one view from its single window.

This is not the case with Iain Crichton Smith. There are superficial similarities. Living in Oban, he like Brown seems to be choosing remoteness as a necessary condition for his work; like Brown he moves easily from poetry to fiction. A frequent theme of his poetry and fiction—especially in *Consider the Lilies* (1968)—is, like Brown, a deep concern with the way in which the past of Scotland, and especially its bleak religious history, has malformed the present. But a closer examination of *Consider the Lilies* reveals their basic difference.

The novel tells of old Mrs Scott, a Lewis woman who is being put out of her house at the time of the Clearances. Having all her life conformed to the joyless demands of her religion, with all the concomitant respect for Authority and Law that that conformity implies, she is therefore thrown into total confusion at her church's failure to support her in what she sees as her right to remain. The theme thereafter is of her liberation, her regeneration as a free individual, released from the ice of religious repression.

The difference between Smith and Brown emerges through this. For Smith, the individual consciousness, its fulfilment and its pain, is *more* important than the history and the background, whereas for Brown, one is conscious almost always, as in his story of the sacrifice of Earl Magnus, that the individual's importance is as a part in the heraldic unity of Land and Sea, Birth and Death, History and the Present. And Smith in his following novels and stories was to reveal an almost embarrassing honesty about himself through his projections of what he so patently felt as personal issues in *The Last Summer* (1969), a Lewis adolescence, drawing, one feels, much on autobiography, and showing the author's love-hate relationship with images of beauty, power, accompanying evil. In *My Last Duchess* (1971), *The Black and the Red* (1973) (a collection of fine short stories haunted by Smith's feeling for a lost and nobler way of life, as in the story "Under an American Sky") and *Goodbye Mr Dixon* (1974) Smith continued to confess his own agonies of unsureness about personal relations—and the question of their ultimate significance.

But for all the agonising, wholeness of self is Smith's overall concern, as with Brown; although Smith's journey is a more tortuous one than Brown's. *Goodbye Mr Dixon* marks a farewell to some of his dead selves, but no final resting place has been reached.

With *Docherty* (1975) William McIlvanney immediately asserted his place at the head of modern Scottish fiction. *Remedy is None* (1966) has won him the Geoffrey Faber Memorial Award for 1967; but looking back at that novel the impression overall is of uncontrolled hatred of a system which stifled the potential of the working class. Young Charlie's blind violence as he lashes out against the suffocating bourgeoisie becomes tedious. But the novel has real power and nobility, and as with Sharp, Brown and Smith, the concern is with regeneration. Charlie is brought to see that his society (West of Scotland industrial) needs charity and integrity above all; violent and hateful attitudes cannot be cured with violence and hate. A similar concern with integrity filled *A Gift from Nessus* (1968), but I feel this was a difficult second novel to write, which rarely broke out of the conventional pattern of, say, Amis's *That Uncertain Feeling*. Perhaps McIlvanney saw this as he shifted ground to write poetry and drama—and *Docherty*. Here is the hatred of the system, only distanced and tempered with outstanding humour, directly in line from Gibbon's use of "the speak" in *A Scots Quair*. Magnificently McIlvanney evokes Graithnock, a Kilmarnock-like mining town, in 1914; its chat, its smells, its green surroundings—and its High Street, with the Docherty family, of Irish origin, as focus. Docherty is the father—and he is one of the great creations of Scottish fiction—different from, say, Gourlay of *The House with the Green Shutters*, or Chris Guthrie of *A Scots Quair*, but comparable as an epic figure of complete integrity realised with truth and consistency.

Very different in scale and approach, but comparable in the sheer sincerity and dignity of its aim is John Herdman's *A Truth Lover* (1973). For all the apparent difference of type and class between Docherty the miner and Duncan Straiton, the young misanthrope who caustically surveys Scottish bigotry and pomposity, both are concerned with fundamentals of wholeness and honesty, and with the difficulty of asserting these in an alien and hostile society, and both novels succeed in presenting us with a central figure of impressive integrity. And equally concerned with the possibility of wholeness within a Scottish society which makes that wholeness elusive are two novelists whose gentleness and sensitivity of response seems to me to have caused the full significance and beauty of this fiction to be neglected. Nancy Brysson Morrison, whose work dates back to the fertile 'thirties with her superb *The Gowk Storm* (1933), created deceptively gentle tales of family crises set against lyrically evoked and ever-changing Scottish landscapes; tales which slowly gathered immense power through their beautifully structured anticipations and echoes, as in *The Winnowing Years* (1949), a chronicle of several centuries of life in a manse, or *The Other Traveller* (1957), a Gunn-like situation where a man scarred by marriage misfortune achieves peace and wholeness in a timeless Scottish country setting. Her great strengths are her feeling for landscape and history, and her ability to convey the sense of a timeless, yet real, community. If she has a weakness, it is that her overt Christianity, like Mackay Brown's, becomes intrusive and at odds with the real aesthetic shape of her work; which does not happen in the work of Ian Niall, probably best known for his non-fiction naturalist works like *The Poacher's Handbook* (1946) and *A Fowler's World* (1968). But in the 'sixties he began a series of the gentlest of fictions about the lives of archetypal country figures with *The Country Blacksmith* (1966), *The Galloway Shepherd* (1970), *The Village Policeman* (1971) and *The Forester* (1972). His stories hardly seem fictions at all, but are completely convincing and have a simplicity and dignity of statement which only Mackay Brown can rival, sharing too Brown's deep concern with the passing of older, rural values, but accepting this with a greater serenity.

In rounding off this description of what I feel to be the noblest and most ambitious Scottish fiction, I would like to pay special tribute to the work of two of the great figures of the renaissance of the 'twenties and 'thirties, whose major work does appear to lie in that period, but whose later work continues to surprise and delight in its constant change and fertility of approach. Sadly, Eric Linklater died recently. In tracing the development of his work in the 'fifties and 'sixties, I was struck by the movement in the 'fifties into a kind of wry cynicism, which although it never lost its redeeming love of wit and grotesque humour, was a dark period for the buoyant optimist of *Magnus Merriman* (1934) and the *Juan* novels (*Juan in America* (1931) and *Juan in China* (1937)).

> We who are the shrivelled little bastard cousins of God—the last thin paring of his finger nails, with the urge to create still beating against the hard and horny consciousness of separation from him . . . We, like God, need belief . . . God himself is failing, and if scepticism, neglect, and blank indifference can undo Him how shall I be immune?

This was in *A Sociable Plover* (1957). The mood came to a comic, sardonic, bleak head in *The Merry Muse* (1959) with the death of its likeable, vivid poet Hector McRae in the most absurd of Edinburgh road accidents. Linklater seemed to have reached a kind of middle-aged desolation of spirit. *Position at Noon* (1958) was only a tired echo of the Juan novels and *Roll of Honour* (1961) is haunted by a middle-aged fatalism. All the more marvellous was the resurgence then of exploration in *A Man over Forty* (1964) and in particular, the brave, bizarre, and disturbing *A Terrible Freedom* (1966). Here Linklater moved into what was for him a new, disturbing area—the landscape of dreams. Freedom in that landscape is terrible for Linklater and his ageing protagonist, Evan Gaffikin; but it releases in this novel scenes of startling new beauty, with a power that even Linklater hadn't touched before. It also raised, for the first time in his work, that ultimate question which the sceptic in him had always avoided—the metaphysical enquiry about man's final spiritual self, underlying the surface, comic behaviour which had so occupied his satiric view hitherto. Thus—although no answers are suggested beyond some persuasive and beautiful glimpses—Linklater seems to me to have joined with Muir and Gunn in the highest quest of Scottish fiction.

The other great tradition of Scottish fiction I isolated was that of bitter, denigratory comment on what most of the practitioners of this kind see as a sick Scotland; a tradition which goes back to Scott's *Waverley*. Undoubtedly the greatest figure here for sheer range and massive achievement is Robin Jenkins.

Jenkins has been writing since *So Gaily Sings the Lark* (1950). He has written nearly twenty novels—none of them anything other than deeply serious and sometimes agonisingly harsh studies of love, whether it be family love or the love of a vision, a personal aspiration which may turn out to be an illusion, but which is the intense reality for its suffering holder. A fine critic of Jenkins, Alistair Thompson, thought that for all the suffering in the novels, Jenkins presented love as an epiphany, a redeeming affirmation. But with the benefit of looking over a greater range of his work, I feel that Jenkins's progress has been away from the theme of redemption and possible attainment of wholeness to a negative vision. Consider how the message of an early novel, the study of the poor boy John Stirling striving to be educated, dreaming of release through the traditional Scottish educational egalitarianism, *Happy for the Child* (1953) is reversed in the later study of an Eastern boy's similar dream in *The Holy Tree* (1969). In the first John Stirling achieves peace and union with his mother, and a quiet hope ends the book—but murder and desolation end the boy's dream in *The Holy Tree*. The comic atmosphere of earlier novels like *The Thistle and the Grail* (1954), with its greater affection for small town character in its quest for reflected football glory, or the hope of regenerating dead love presented in *Love is a Fervent Fire* (1959) become fused in the bitter parody of each in *A Very Scotch Affair* (1969) where a Scotsman—whose name Mungo argues his stereotype role—is bitterly observed failing to find this dream, amidst some very nastily and convincingly dissected neighbours. But indeed Jenkins' affirmative attitudes were questionable from the beginning. Although the eastern novels like *Dust on the Paw* (1961) and *Some Kind of Grace* (1960) seem to hold out a possible charity, can one ever banish that horrifying, tragic and magnificent picture of the slum child who hangs himself as he sees his dreams vanish at the end of *The Changeling* (1958)? And although there are fine, enduring women like Mrs McShelvie of *Guests of War* (1956) whom Thompson rightly compares as achievement with Jeanie Deans and Chris Guthrie, can such occasional figures like her and the martyr figure McInver of *The Missionaries* (1957) really atone for the devastating pictures of human corruption and ant-like insignificance as in that superbly symbolic picture of innocence murdered, *The Conegatherers* (1935)? Jenkins is ultimately, I would argue, a profound and lonely pessimist, in the way of Hardy. He is also a writer of power and symbolism unequalled for its sheer intensity and stamina in all Scottish fiction, although his latest novels and stories from *The Expatriates* (1970), *A Far Cry from Bowmore* (1973) to *A Toast for the Lord* (1973) and *A Figure of Fun* (1975), though as evocative of landscape and setting and loneliness as ever, seem tired compared to those of 1955-65. Perhaps indeed his pessimism has taken its toll.

Certainly after the war there was a deep sense of disillusion and elegy to be found throughout Scottish fiction—for example, J. D. Scott's deceptively quiet analysis of three lovers, set against a crumbling old Scottish house, *The End of An Old Song* (1954). It takes time to realise that this delicate and merciless picture of middle-class rural Scottish life is in fact not only an immediate human situation, but a strange kind of allegory for Scottish character and history—the title is deliberately an echo of the words which pronounced a death-knell for a very deep part of the Scottish identity in 1707. Directly comparable with this novel, of lacking its beautiful sense of place, are two more recent works, two of the most important of Scottish novels, James Kennaway's *Household Ghosts* (1961) and Muriel Spark's *The Prime of Miss Jean Brodie* (1961). Unusual in Scottish fiction, they deal with the middle and upper classes of Scotland, their poisonous charms and hypocrisies, with rare satirical edge. Both are deeply enigmatic, not to say ambiguous, in their attribution of guilt and responsibility, and both in their settings have a deep awareness of a black, Calvinist bias to their strange central characters. Kennaway's is the darker, probably the most bitter of all modern Scottish novels, following his already bitter picture of Scots character in the hard drinking and dual-natured colonel of *Tunes of Glory* (1956). *Household Ghosts*, in its story of the dour teacher Dow destroying lovely and impulsive Mary and her brother, re-enacts the story of Knox and Mary. His achievement is to make the two levels of history and Scottish "ghosts" on one hand completely compatible with the modern, real picture of a disintegrating marriage on the other. Similarly Muriel Spark manages to present Jean Brodie as a twentieth century Scottish teacher trying new methods in a hostile grey Edinburgh on one hand, but also as the descendant of infamous Deacon Brodie, on the other. Scotland's past lives in these fascinating and ambiguous central figures.

Different from these subtle descriptions of middle class betrayal, but similar in its overall bitter view of Scottish life, is the tradition of *No Mean City*, in which the writer turns his attention to the obvious blight of city life in Glasgow and the big cities. Edward Gaitens wrote the most powerful of the post-war indictments in *The Dance of the Apprentices* (1946). Here, though written with power and lyric ability, is the tendency to stereotype so common in the Glasgow novel, in the picture of sensitive Francie McDonnell, doomed with his friends to find his socialist ideals wither in a Glasgow dominated by Capital. The conclusion sets the tone for the Glasgow novel of the next twenty years, as Francie broods in the cell to which conscientious objection has taken him . . .

Never would he in the humblest of ways be a leader of men. He would daydream . . . till advancing years deadened his power of dreaming, and he would end like his father and brothers, an obscure walker in the drama of life.

The tendency to melodrama, the pessimism, and the barely-controlled anger are the hallmark of this flourishing, if negative, tradition; and the work of A. J. Cronin (*Hatter's Castle* (1931)), Fred Urquart (*Time Will Knit* (1938)), George Blake (*The Shipbuilders* (1935)), and Lennox Kerr (*Glenshiels* (1932)) has been carried on by many more than Jenkins; outstandingly, by James Allan Ford, George Friel, Archie Hind, Alistair Mair, Stuart MacGregor, Allan Campbell McLean, Angus Wolfe Murray, John Quigley and Hugh C. Rae.

Ford's *A Statue for a Public Place* (1965) and *A Judge of Men* (1968) are fine, satiric novels which look in turn at the lives of an eminent Scottish civil servant and a famous Scottish Law Lord. In the latter particularly Ford analyses keenly and honestly the ambiguities of public and private morality which cause the destruction of self of Robert Falkland, an achievement in fiction which can stand being set beside Stevenson's *Weir of Hermiston*. Scotland is seen through bleak, though not embittered, lenses here—as in the work of Glasgow schoolteacher George Friel, which seems to me to be some of the finest and most skilfully crafted of modern Scottish fiction. It is a shame and blot on our national self respect that his death last year should have gone unremarked and unlamented. For creative ability and sensitivity Friel had no superior, and his handful of bleak, experimental and highly poetic novels should be compulsory reading for all interested in Scottish culture. His *The Bank of Time* (1959) was a "first novel" choice by Hutchinson's; while his strange, sad study of the predestined failure of a slum child with visions in *The Boy Who Wanted Peace* (1964) was successfully dramatised on television. *Grace and Miss Partridge* (1969) continued to explore, with the most delicate balance of wry humour and savage satire, the flatness and hopelessness of slum life, with an increase in the use of brilliant techniques of juxtaposition of fast moving, contrasting episodes which nevertheless fused together in the denouement. Friel's undoubted masterpiece, the comic, horrific indictment of not just Scottish but universal life and attitudes to children and education in the modern wilderness, is *Mr Alfred M.A.* (1972). Mr Alfred is a sensitive, shy teacher, broken in dreams of being a poet, unable to teach with the saving shell of personal toughness and ultimate disinterest of his colleagues, who hold him in mild contempt. Friel's achievement is to explore Alfred's mind till we see indeed that he possessed the truth, that he is the lost awareness which sees the writing on the wall (the novel was originally to be called *The Writing on the Wall*), the wrecked lives in the squalid schemes, the cheapness of the media, the shallowness of our institutions. His last novel was *An Empty House* (1974); he is an immeasurable loss to Scottish literature.

Archie Hind has written one novel and promised so much more. His *The Dear Green Place* (1968) is an evocation of Glasgow by its hero, a struggling young office worker who wants to create. Poetical, feeling and alive to the paradoxes of Glasgow as few other novels are, nevertheless the novel seems to me to be unresolved, with an unconvincing ending and—bane of other good writers like MacIlvanney and Sharp—often, in its honest desire to avoid cliché, lapsing into the purple and the pretentious. So does Alistair Mair's *The Ripening Time* (1970), which, for all its deep sense of Glasgow materialism and sterility, often approaches pathos as it introduces its bizarre sexual diversions which seem to have been included to guarantee its paperback future. For all its faults, though, important fiction—as is Stuart MacGregor's work, unfortunately limited to two novels by his tragic death in 1973. *The Myrtle and Ivy* (1967) and *The Sinner* (1973) cast a bitter eye at the modern Edinburgh scene; while Allan Campbell McLean's Arts Council Award winner *The Glasshouse* (1969) is a brutal, compulsive study through a young Scottish soldier of army cruelty which puts him high in this group, as does Angus Wolfe Murray's *The End of Something Nice* (1967), a chilling tale told with deceptive simplicity, about the separation of a brother and sister who are unnaturally close—possibly as a result of the neglect of their upper-class parents and teachers. Murray satirises here the same levels of Scottish society as James Kennaway in *Household Ghosts*; it is sad that he has not yet followed up this satiric promise. In a way this is also true of the work of John Quigley—who has a good five novels since his first, *To Remember with Tears* (1963), but who seems to me to have lost the commitment and intensity which filled the first. In the bleak, tragi-comic story of the old crofter Cruachan Campbell, a lonely, stubborn relic of a by-gone age and a dying community, there was something of Mackay Brown's *Greenvoe*, and the bitter humour of Friel's *Mr Alfred M.A.* Albeit sometimes melodramatic, Quigley's aims and achievement in this novel were of the highest order, as in his later, bleak novels which moved into more fashionable, less explicitly Scottish situations like those of journalism (*The Bitter Lollipop*, 1964) or the whisky business (*The Secret Soldier*, 1966). His most important work yet is the drawing of the typical, dour, materialist David Dron, directly in the tradition of Gourlay of *The House with the Green Shutters*, in a novel of sordid Glasgow in buildings and business, *The Golden Stream* (1970). *King's Royal* (1976) is twice as long as his first novel, apparently epic in scale, but with a curious flat echo of the George Blake chronicles of West Coast families, without, say, the acid edge of Guy MacCrone at his caustic best on the Glasgow middle classes in *Wax Fruit* (1947), that impressive trilogy on the social aspirations of the Moorhouse family. McCrone increasingly seems to me to be under-estimated—possibly because his satire on the snobberies and foibles of his protagonists is tempered by a charitable acceptance that Glasgow did become great through just such a mixture of vision and petty ambition in its merchants—and their wives. In any case, his trilogy and descendants like *Aunt Bel* (1949), *The Hayburn Family* (1952), *James and Charlotte* (1955), and *An Independent Young Man* (1961), however happily they resolve their immediate personal problems, nevertheless leave a serious, ironic overall picture of a Glasgow which may change superficially, but continues to be grey, conservative, and pretty unconcerned about the larger issues of the arts, the outside world and liberal attitudes.

But the tradition of *No Mean City* (1935), of the naturalistic, bittersweet, raw Scottish industrial novel continues unabated—so much so that one feels that the stereotypes are now a serious danger to the novelist. They spoiled some of Hind's *The Dear Green Place*, much of Quigley's work, most of Hugh Munro's *The Clydesiders* (1961), Alexander Highland's *The Dark Horizon* (1971), to mention only some of the artistically better examples of the type. It is now almost impossible to "see" the urban scene with clear eyes; which makes it all the more astonishing when the feat is achieved, as in Alexander Trocchi's poetic evocation of loneliness, the factory-and-canal desolation of Lowland Scotland, *Young Adam* (1961). Here is an evocation of moral alienation with its roots shown to be deep in a spiritual sickness which is Scottish—and quite credible, as the novel's "justified sinner" moves towards the terrible climax, where another man hangs for his crime, and the sinner's moral awareness is shown to be quite arid and dead. It's interesting that this process of total moral degeneration should be the theme of Gordon Williams' first and only explicitly Scottish novel, *From Scenes Like These* (1968), the description of the making of a basically healthy and sensitive boy into a brute mind, bellowing aggressively at the ritual release of the football match at the end. Williams has moved outwards into novels about the RAF (*The Camp*, 1967) about journalists in England (*The Upper Pleasure Garden*, 1970) and America (*Walk Don't Walk*, 1972), but it is interesting that in all these novels it is still a specifically Scottish consciousness, a Scottish central character, who is measuring himself against the broader experience —as in the violent novel of Ian McGraw from Shettleston in London crime, *Big Morning Blues* (1974). A similar interest in the analysis of violence in terms of Scottish experience has been even more extensively developed in the work of Hugh C. Rae, whose vivid *Skinner* (1965), based on the multiple murderer Manuel, succeeded in transcending the limits of the crime novel, as did many of his later works in the genre; *Night Pillow* (1967), the story of a family feud after a rape, which showed, like Williams's work, the connection between the sordid action and the debased Scottish environment of the housing schemes; *A Few Small Bones* (1968); *The Marksman* (1971); and especially *The Saturday Epic* (1970), which attempted to portray much more than Rae had hitherto tried, broadening its view to recreate the motivation of two Glasgow gangs. Although touched by melodrama, it showed Rae to be developing into an important Scottish novelist.

In listing these examples of response to the negatives of Scottish life I am aware of the dangers of falsifying the scene. Nevertheless it is true, for whatever it is worth, that the strongest modern tradition is a bleak, satiric one; and that there is a real difficulty for the Scottish writer who seeks to find real comedy in such scenes, apart from the ironic and absurd. Nevertheless a few writers succeed, to an extent—notably Chaim Bermant, George MacDonald Fraser and Cliff Hanley. Bermant's *Jericho Sleep Alone* (1964) traces the adolescence of a young Glasgow Jew in a city pleasant with trees and art galleries—another side to our previous view; and sympathises with his ludicrous setbacks with real humour, as in *Ben Preserve Us* (1965)—but isn't it significant that the humour of the second is based on the pawky incidents of a provincial wee town? Bermant has *had* to change his scene to preserve the humour—and later novels move outside Scotland and lose their artistic achievement, which is a shame in that the writer of the poignant *Diary of an Old Man* (1966), a first hand account of old age, has a compassion and warmth in that novel which promised great things. Similarly George MacDonald Fraser creates his humour furth of Scotland, in the adventures of his rogue *Flashman* (1969); in dealing with real Scottish life he manages to make the incidents involving gallus, mindless, dirty Private McAuslan in *The General Danced at Dawn* (1970) and *McAuslan in the Rough* (1974), amusing by detaching McAuslan from any kind of real social conditions, and isolating him in the mythical clichés and special conditions of the British Army abroad. More authentic is the humour of Cliff Hanley, who in *Dancing in the Streets* (1958) genuinely touches the real humour of working class family life. In *The Taste of Too Much* (1960) he extended this to the novel, writing a classic account of adolescence and first love in a setting devoid of razors or violence, although still obviously Glasgow. The *Red-Haired Bitch* (1969) continued to find sharp humour in ordinary Glasgow life—here in its schools with some pungent, yet still good-natured criticisms of Scottish teaching, as the headmaster of his school sets out the Scottish orthodoxies—"Beatles, and guitars, and drugs, and promiscuous sex—they all go together, but not in my school." But for me the funniest Hanley achievement paradoxically illustrates my case that *real* Scottish life is not suitable material for comic fiction is *The Hot Month* (1967), where Hanley's send-up of an untypically hot summer in a West Highland village creates marvellous humour. But although there are some real ironies about the Anglicised gentry, the locals, and West Highland life, the novel is basically escapist in its creation of a bizarre holiday world, and none the worse for that; but in order to achieve its limited humorous effect, like so much of sentimental or even simply pleasant kailyard or melodramatic Scottish fiction, like the work of Jane Duncan, or Lilian Beckwith, or Patrick O'Connor, M. O'Donaghue, Margaret Davies or Robert Crichton it has to limit or falsify the Scottish experience. The stereotypes of *No Mean City* and the Kailyard still flourish.

In having so far described two traditions of Scottish fiction I am aware that in the case of many fine and established Scottish writers I have begged the question by leaving them out of either. This is especially true of a group whose best work seems to me to have been written before the war, but who continued to write thereafter. I have already paid tribute to Naomi Mitchison's *The Bull Calves* (1947); but she continued to write fine children's stories, a comic novel rather like *The Hot Month, Lobsters on the Agenda* (1952) a fine book of Scottish short stories, *Five Men and A Swan* (1957), a science fiction novel (*Memoirs of a Space Woman*, 1962), novels and studies of her beloved Bakgatla tribe of Africa, as well as autobiography. She continues to write original and vivid short stories for the annual collections sponsored for the Scottish Arts Council. But nevertheless, while acknowledging her immense and richly diverse achievement, I feel that her major work in Scottish fiction culminated in *The Bull Calves*, as I feel A. J. Cronin's did in *Hatter's Castle* (1931), Fionn McColla's (Tom MacDonald, who died recently) in *And the Cock Crew* (1945), although some stimulating thought appeared in *At the Sign of the Clenched Fist* (1967) and *Too Long in this Condition* (1975). Likewise George Blake, Bruce Marshal, March Cost, Fred Urquhart, to name a few—but their post-war work lacked the creative surge and ambition of the 'thirties.

Over and above this there are four groups of fiction which for convenience and on a fairly arbitrary basis I have separated from the two main traditions, even although one might well decide to replace them in these traditions. Firstly there is the strong Scottish tradition of historical and adventure writing, of which the outstanding modern representatives are Nigel Tranter and Dorothy Dunnett. The first has set himself more epic and demanding tasks than ever before, and performed them with dignity and success, in his Robert Bruce trilogy, *The Steps to the Empty Throne* (1969-71), and *The Wallace* (1975), while Dorothy Dunnett has just completed the six novels of her *The Game of Kings* series. Here, in the person of her resourceful, suave, dangerous hero Francis Crawford of Lymond, is a James Bond of the Middle Ages, set in a thoroughly researched and vividly presented historical background. And these two are backed by many able recreaters of history—to name only a few, Marion Campbell, Jane Lane, Jane Oliver, Elizabeth Sutherland. And akin to them are the many writers of soundly constructed adventure and thriller novels, from Sacha Carnegie and Henry Calvin (Cliff Hanley) to Alistair McLean and Josephine Tay.

The second group is small, but fascinating. It contains those who use the more experimental forms of the novel to explore themes which may be Scottish, but which oddly enough seem ultimately to share a strange atmosphere of a geographical and spiritual No Man's Land—as though the experimental methods had been adopted as necessary for investigation of strangely alienated people in dreamlike landscapes. To break my own definition as soon as it is made, Sydney Goodsir Smith's *Carotid Cornucopius* (1964), his Rabelaisian, Joycean account in rich Scots of the "splores, cantraips, wisdoms, houghmagandies, peribibulatiouns and all kinna abstrapulous junketings" of the Caird of the Cannon Gait is rooted solidly in Edinburgh and Scotland and in, as Hugh MacDiarmid says "the recaptured spirit of Dunbar, Sir Thomas Urquhart and Burns," however fantastic the ongoings may—and do—become. It stands alone; very different from the quiet, disturbing work of Elspeth Davie, whose short stories *The Spark* (1968) and *The High Tide Talker* (1976), and her novels *Providings* (1965) and *Creating a Scene* (1971) explore the apparently mundane from a curiously and effectively detached angle that paradoxically conveys an immense, distanced sympathy for her meticulously observed protagonists. Without her restrained power, but similarly exploring the ordinary from a highly personal point of view is John Elliott's first novel, *Another Example of Indulgence* (1970), while Sheila MacLeod continues to convey intense experience of loneliness and breakdown through unique style in *The Moving Accident* (1967), *The Snow-White Soliloquies* (1970), and *Letters from the Portuguese* (1971). Robert Nye is English, but has lived and worked so long in Scotland that it would be petty not to mention his ambitious, difficult, but impressive novel *Doubtfire* (1967) and his delightful, whimsical, learned fantasies, *Tales I Told My Mother* (1969), together with his bawdy, huge, highly acclaimed recreation of the life of *Falstaff* (1976). His friend and collaborator William Watson has also written a complex and funny love story, *Better than One* (1969).

This does not exhaust Scottish experimentation, and I use one of the most notable of Scottish writers of "speculative fiction" as he calls it to make the transition to my third remaining group, that summed up by the unsatisfying, necessary label "Anglo-Scots." By this I mean those who live and work outside Scotland and whose work is primarily for a British or international market, whose themes are universal and whose settings non-Scottish. Giles Gordon has now a distinguished body of such fiction, including *Pictures From an Exhibition* (1970), *Farewell Fond Dreams* (1975) (both collections of short stories), and the novels, *About a Marriage* (1972) and *Scenes of Married Life* (1976). But the outstanding Scottish writers furth of Scotland have undoubtedly been James Kennaway and Muriel Spark—whose work on Scottish themes has already been discussed, but whose main work lies in a broader tradition of fiction. In their own separate and varied ways they are very much experimentalists too—witness Kennaway's diversity of techniques in *Some Gorgeous Accident* (1967) and *The Cost of Living Like This* (1969) and Spark's changes in styles from, say, the fairly conventional in *The Mandelbaum Gate* (1965) to *The Driver's Seat* (1970) or *The Takeover* (1976). And, for the rest of the "Anglo-Scots," impressive work has been produced by George Beardmore, Campbell Black, Hugo Charteris, Walker Hamilton, Elizabeth Mavor, Rosemary and Shena MacKay, Pauline Neville and Ian Sinclair.

Finally, the short story. Many of the writers already mentioned, like Mackay Brown or Elspeth Davie, are primarily masters of this form. In addition the work of some specialists remains to be mentioned; Tom Hanlon (*Once in Every Lifetime*, 1945), Dorothy Haynes (*Thou Shalt not Suffer a Witch*, 1949), G. F. Hendry (*The Blackbird of Ospro*, 1945), Morley Jamieson (*The Old Wife*, 1972), Eona McNicol (*The Hallowe'en Hero*, 1969), and outstandingly, Fred Urquhart's magnificent two volume collection, *The Dying Stallion* (1967), and *The Ploughing Match* (1968). In terms of general collections since the war there has been *No Scottish Twilight* (1947) edited by Maurice Lindsay and Fred Urquhart; the Faber book of *Scottish Short Stories* of 1932 updated and revised by Fred Urquhart in 1957; the World's Classics *Scottish Short Stories* (1963) edited by J. M. Reid; and J. F. Hendry's second collection for Penguin (the first in 1943), *Scottish Short Stories* (1970) and *Ten Modern Scottish Short Stories* (1973), edited by Robert Millar and John Low. In addition, the Scottish Arts Council have since 1973 sponsored an annual collection of *Scottish Short Stories*; four have appeared to date.

Scottish Poetry in English

IAIN CRICHTON SMITH

The period since the war has been a rich one for Scottish poetry though no poet of major status has emerged. (I exclude Hugh MacDiarmid because his best work was written before the war; also that best work was in Scots). I suppose that in the period immediately after the war the dominant Scottish poet writing in English was Edwin Muir. It seems to me now however that, perhaps as a result of the decline in what might be called the classical tradition, his poetry on the whole appears to be less interesting than it was. It is possible that his poems about Time and labyrinths and Troy and Hector will not be considered important in the future but rather that individual poems like *The Horses* (the one about the atomic war), certain of his poems about Scotland, some of his love poems and ballads, a poem like *The Combat* (which is not so explicit as some of his other work) and a poem like *Merlin* will survive. Many of these poems have a rhythmical and linguistic vitality which is lacking in some of his more philosophical poems some of which could do with a greater degree of concrete particularity. This lack of particularity seems to me to be a very great weakness of his poetry and a surprising one since Kafka whom he studied so much knew the importance of particularity.

A poet against whom this charge could not be made is Norman MacCaig who has been a dominating influence since about 1955 with his first book of real importance *Riding Lights*. MacCaig's strength has always been in his particularity and his imaginative creation of radiant objects. It is also the case however that, perhaps in order to lend intellectual respectability to his descriptive world, he has been addicted to philosophical and metaphysical speculation which sometimes spoils his poetry. He does not (unlike Wallace Stevens) have a metaphysical mind, but rather a poetic one.

Thus lines like the following are exact and brilliant:

> A hen stares at nothing with one eye
> and then picks it up.

29

But then later on in the same poem he writes a line like the following:

Self within self, a pile of selves I stand

which is awkward speculation which doesn't fit in well with the rest of the poem "Summer Farm." A poem like "Water Tap" however is all of a piece and quite sparkling and vital.

It might in his earlier work have been said of him that he was more interested in lochs and mountains than he was in people. However in recent years he has characters other than himself in his poems, characters who are seen in their frayed humanity.

It seems to me that in many ways MacCaig has been one of the most interesting poets to have written in Scotland since the war and one of the few poets to have had a truly poetic mind and imagination.

One of my own favourite poets since I first read *Sea Talk* has been George Bruce. The clipped nature of his language in that book seems to me to represent exactly the area about which he is writing—Aberdeen and the North East, which he calls "the land without myth." Since then however he has extended his range and I feel that his most successful poems have been personal ones, especially love poems.

Thus I consider "Three Love Poems For My Wife" to be an excellent achievement and especially the second poem in the group which has a great pathos and depth of feeling. I am not so happy about his social poems (though his social conscience has led him to write such poems) nor am I happy with his poems about Glasgow. His language doesn't seem to me to fit such a swarming city. But in the broken language of his love poems for his wife I think he has found a new notation which could be profitably extended. I feel that the strength of his kind of poetry has always lain in lack of explicitness, in tautness, rather than in expansiveness.

The phenomenon loosely described as Edwin Morgan (it is possible that there may be five of them, one of them concrete) has erupted in so many directions simultaneously that it is difficult to write about him briefly. However, apart from his concrete poetry and his translations (both of which I am incompetent to speak about with author ty) one can distinguish poems of reportage, SF poems, poems about Glasgow, love poems and other poems not so easily classified.

I do not like his poems about Marilyn Monroe and Edith Piaf since they seem to me to be superficial and in places exclamatory. Nor am I a great admirer of his instamatic poems since the poetry there is too close to notes.

Clever as he is (and I am often reminded of Auden in thinking about him) I must say that I prefer those poems of his which show deep feeling. Some of the love poems I feel however are too naive. Poems however like "Glasgow Green" I like very much indeed. But much more profoundly than these I like certain poems which have great depth of feeling combined with a linguistic strangeness which I find refreshing. I like for instance a poem like "Absence" very much. In this poem he is writing of himself as alone in a room in London and he says:

> My shadow, do you hear the streets?
> Are you at my heels? Are you here?
> And I throw back the sheets.

There is no question but that Morgan has a remarkable ability to create strange ghosts out of the everyday in a warm, human yet purely poetic language. For an intellect so richly endowed this is a very precious achievement.

Morgan I suppose is at the opposite pole to someone like George Mackay Brown who turns ever more and more obsessively the world of Orkney to the light of his mind and whose sympathies are not with the future but rather with the past (in this connection my own sympatheis are more with Morgan than with Brown).

Mackay Brown has developed a definite style of his own, sometimes spare, sometimes ornate and sometimes very mannered with references to apparently random numbers and to words like "honey." However, all that said, he has written some very fine moving poems such as for instance "Wedding" which has great pathos and mystery. It is interesting that he chose a solution different from Edwin Muir's. Whereas Muir's speculative mind, addicted to myth, left the local to a great extent for the world of Europe and especially Greece, Mackay Brown has remained true to the local and the particular and in this lies a great part of his strength. His Catholic faith has given him a stationary gravity and a confident consistency in his own area of discourse, though perhaps the "centre" of a poet like MacCaig is a more truly poetic one.

Whenever one thinks of Scottish poetry one nearly always thinks of poets who have spent their creative lives in Scotland. But of course there have been and are poets who may be called Scottish but who do not live in Scotland. I am thinking in particular of W. S. Graham: and I also refer to the late Burns Singer. However, both poets are connected in one's mind since both had an obsession and that obsession was language. Graham, I think, quite obviously influenced Singer though essentially

31

their poetry is quite different. Singer seems to have had a driving forceful omniscient mind impatient with the second-rate, European in some of its preconceptions, and aggressive and perfectionist in his work. He was probably the most ambitious of our poets since MacDiarmid (who has written preceptively of him). Graham of course came to prominence earlier. His early work has an orchestral music almost immune to the intelligence but very strange and poetic. In later years he has simplified his poetry but perhaps in the process has made it too cold and intellectual. My own feeling with him as with Singer is that his preoccupation with language (considered as a subject) has been harmful to his work. (It seems sometimes as if Scottish poets have this obsession with metaphysics as if by some Calvinist masochism they were trying to compensate for writing poetry at all). Those poems of Graham's which are situated most firmly in time and place, such as his poems about his childhood in Greenock, seem to me to be his best. His series of "Letters" and one or two of his ballads are very fine and the music though sparser permits an entry for the intelligence. I do not have such a high regard for *The Nightfishing* as some critics have: it seems to me that his linguistic speculations spoil some of the most marvellously descriptive and tactile passages. But he is obviously a poet of a very high order.

I think that Burns Singer's mind was the more powerful of the two in a philosophical or metaphysical manner. His early poems are by far his best: in his later work he becomes too abstract, a dangerous weakness (though it does not seem to spoil Empson's poetry). He wrote a number of long poems, among them "The Transparent Prisoner," a very ambitious poem which though interesting I do not find entirely convincing. His *Sonnets To A Dying Man* also have a great deal of passion but are spoilt by an almost Elizabethan bravado which seems slightly odd now. I think, as with Graham (and for that matter with MacCaig) that his simplest poems are very often his best. For instance, I am very fond of "Peterhead In May," a beautiful painting-like poem, cool and elegant, and not without metaphysical implication. His best poem, I think, is his "Marcus Aurelius," a fairly long poem about power which I find totally convincing and linguistically fascinating as in the lines:

> A mind erratic within
> his decent body carries
> piecemeal a soul which cannot live outside.

In "Peterhead In May" his imagery is unusual and very different from MacCaig's, *e.g.*

32

A beam cool as a butler
steps from the lighthouse

My own feeling is that Burns Singer (what a name for a poet!) was a poet of spectacular gifts: a reassessment of his work is long overdue.

Maurice Lindsay is a poet who has written with great fluency and much variety for a long time. I must say that I find his poetry about human beings more satisfying than his nature poetry such as "At The Mouth Of The Ardyne." A poem like "Love's Anniversaries" is very warm and open to the world in which he lives, to its vulnerable emotions and accidents, and he has recorded many moments of that world. As he himself writes in a poem "Written At Hans Christian Andersen's Birth-place:"

The whole of this terrible tiny world might be
dismissed as a beautiful madman's dream but that each of us knows
whenever we move out from the warmth of our loneliness
we may be wearing the Emperor's new clothes.

In Glasgow too—where Lindsay lives—there has emerged in recent years a kind of poetry which speaks the voice of the city as in the work of Stephen Mulrine and Tom Leonard. "The Coming Of The Wee Malkies," in its zany menacing eeriness, seems to fit in perfectly well with the world of Billy Connolly as lately revealed. "The Good Thief," another classic of the genre, is based on a very fine idea and a very Glasgow one. I have also seen the style applied to translations of Catullus but am not sure whether the work of the Latin poet has not been made too pawky. I would like to see the style and techniques applied in a more extended manner to more serious and larger subjects to really gauge their true potential. However I feel that Mulrine and Leonard have already used Glasgow speech in a more vital way than Edwin Morgan does for example in "Good Friday" where his ventriloquism has momently deserted him.

Very far from these poets in technique is D. M. Black, a virtuoso who may in certain ways owe something to George MacBeth. For certainly like Macbeth he has a cool way with words, an interest in form, a somewhat clinical approach to subject matter, and often weird macabre topics. In some of his more immediately accessible poems like "The Educators" he makes great fun of the educational establishment (in a very different way from Robert Garioch, for example) but in poems like "The Red Judge" and "The Ol-mag" and "The Pet Shop" there is a much weirder imagination at work. I should be happier however if the civilised surface of the verse were to crack and a real cry of individual anguish to escape. Hitchcock may be a good director but he's not a great one, and there is a deeper seriousness that a poet must get at.

Another poet who criticises certain aspects of society is Alan Jackson who has already gained immortality with his two-liner "Young Politician" (derived perhaps ultimately from "Holy Willie's Prayer" and substituting politics for religion). "The Worstest Beast" is another of his successful poems. I feel however that in some of his poems his style hasn't quite meshed with the subject matter and if this were to happen often he would be a very powerful poet indeed. It may be that many of his poems need to be read aloud for I have been greatly impressed with him at poetry readings.

Two poets who have a political bias in their work are Tom Buchan and Alan Bold. Buchan is I think stylistically the more extrovert and brutal especially in poems like "President Nixon Announces the U.S. Invasion Of Cambodia on TV." A number of his poems such as for instance "The Flaming Man" are of this indignant kind. "The Low Road" is another poem which deals with roughly similar subject matter though it is more specifically Scottish.

Alan Bold is less brutal (and perhaps less influenced by American poets) in his language and sometimes more close to the world of the ordinary human being, as for instance in his fine paradoxical poem "Cause and Effect:"

> He thought before the war
> of conflicts, heroism, enemies
> who had to be crushed:
> causes that had to be fought for.
>
> He had no time before the war
> for bright skies, fields, the warm
> sun, his woman, only
> causes that had to be fought for.
>
> I see him now after the war
> in my lifetime. I notice his love
> of the sun, bright skies, his woman:
> causes that have to be fought for.

Stewart Conn is not I think a political poet in any significant sense. He shows a love of order informed by feeling in many of his poems and, often, as in poems like "The Clearing" and "The Orchard" a delicacy of form and language. However I believe that his poems about people

34

are his best poems—such poems as "Sisters" and "Summer Afternoon"—as also poems like "Todd" where he draws on his Ayrshire background. One of the poems of his that I like very much is "Arrivals," which ends:

> All we have is each other.
> I sometimes wonder
> if that is enough
> whether being together
> enlarges or diminishes grief.

His delicacy and sparseness of form, often combined with a rich sensuous content, are very moving.

Robin Fulton does not often show sensuousness in his poetry. He is a more philosophical poet than Conn and seems sometimes to be building up reality block by block in a cartesian manner. The stone is a significant symbol in one of his books. Many people may find his poetry too intellectual but I find it exciting and curiously moving. The quality of the mind behind the work is fine and discriminating and as honest as the protagonist in his poem "A Meticulous Observer." His variations on a key image—such as the stone—can be very fertile and thought-provoking.

Giles Gordon is an experimentalist in prose, learning much from the French novel. His poems too are often dry and deliberately unemotional, relying primarily on description. But those poems of his which are formed by passion are the ones I like. A good example is "Elegy *I.M.* Orlando Tobias Gordon" where from the paraphernalia of daily living flatly exposed there emerges something very memorable:

> And they covered your body and hid you
> from me or what you did not wish to see.
> Our world is difficult, short of meaning.
> If there is a God then there is a God,
> To me you are dead. I am so detached
> from you now that I still see you breathing
> in your tent, your perfect features so small
> yet a miniature version of a man.
> Such perfection could not stand our air long.

A poet who made a big impression when his first book came out is Alasdair Maclean. A Highland poet who has yet learned much from Ted Hughes and Norman MacCaig, he might at first sight appear to be over-derivative. This however is not the case as a careful study of "Our Bull" (which might at first sight appear to be a pure Ted Hughes poem) will show. For one thing his statements are plainer than those of Hughes and not so apocalyptic. There is however another side to him, a mysterious eerie side which emerges in poems like "Bathrooms" and "Question And Answer," the latter of which must be the archetypal anti-love poem with its image of the rat:

> Satisfied then you turn your back to sleep
> and I lie awake feeling the taste of the wire
> between my teeth, feeling in the darkness
> the cold water flow over me

I find this unflinching confrontation of reality also in a poem like "A Test of Aloneness." It will be very interesting to see in what direction he will ultimately develop, whether in that of the brutally descriptive or that of the macabre and slightly eerie. One thing is sure, he will never be a romantic poet.

Another poet (and the last I shall speak of) is W. Price Turner who seems to have the same anti-romantic nature as Maclean. Technically, he is as adroit as any of the poets so far discussed and he has in his poetry the curiously wry tone of a man who looks at reality and finds it interesting but rather odd. He is also much more humorous in a sardonic way than Maclean is, as for instance in a poem of his which begins:

> Eight hundred telephone directories
> will bullet-proof a truck, claims
> a fruit company in South America . . .

and ends

> Clearly the moral is to have no truck
> with thick skinned civilisations . . .

having also however traversed the other pun:

> Think of a bullet with so many numbers on it
> stopping nothing

He has in fact a very interesting unconnable mind which is seen at its best in a poem about travelling in another man's car with the other man's wife in it and which ends:

> We'll be free separately soon
> of this shut-in moving mesh
> that has me taking it
> seriously. Here is the tenth commandment
> and this is Bill Turner breaking it.

How much more distant could a poem be than that from the poems that Edwin Muir was writing over thirty years ago!

36

As I reread what I have written I am struck by the extraordinary variety of the poems and poets that I have discussed. Bill Turner is as unlike Edwin Muir as W. S. Graham is unlike Edwin Morgan or as Tom Buchan is unlike George Mackay Brown. Some poets have remained local poets elaborating a limited area: others have spoken with a more international tone. But in general they haven't lost their Scottish resonance which has sometimes emerged as philosophical speculation or plainness of style or unwillingness to say more than can be said. Poets like Robin Fulton have been influenced I think by the minimal poetry of post-war Europe, the approach to silence of writers like Herbert who have engraved their small poems on emptiness.

It seems to me that we should do as we have been doing, that is learn from poets outside our shores though at the same time we should not be slaves of fashion. Nor of course should we forget our own tradition. We must write out of our time and place as honestly as we can. I feel that the kailyard has now gone forever, thanks to MacDiarmid and others. There are minds behind these poems and not simply reflexes. If I hadn't been limited by space I should probably have mentioned other poets such as Andrew Greig: and if I hadn't defined Scottish poets as Scottish by birth I would have mentioned Robert Nye whom I don't think we can claim as our own but who has certainly written some very fine poems indeed. When I think of what has been written in English since the war and add to it what has been written in Gaelic and in Scots, I feel that we have nothing to be ashamed of and a lot to be proud of.

Why Lallans?

ALBERT D. MACKIE

THE QUESTION—why a body of Scottish writers should choose to write in a language likely to condemn them to restricted readership, if not total obscurity—is far from new. "Why write in Lallans?" was asked, in effect, by William Wordsworth when he regretted that Robert Burns had chosen to hide his genius in the "dark lanthorn" of dialect.

Robert Louis Stevenson posed the same question regarding his own poetry in Lallans:

> It's possible—it's hardly mair—
> That some ane, ripin' after lear—
> Some auld professor or young heir,
>   If still there's either—
> May find an' read me, an' be sair
>   Perplexed, puir brither!
>
> *"What tongue does your auld bookie speak?"*
> He'll spier; an' I, his mou to steik:
> *"No bein' fit to write in Greek,*
>   *I wrote in Lallan,*
> *Dear to my heart as the peat reek,*
>   *Auld as Tantallon!*
>
> *"Few spak it than, an' noo there's nane.*
> *My puir auld sangs lie a' their lane,*
> *Their sense, that aince was braw an' plain,*
>   *Tint a' thegither,*
> *Like runes upon a standin' stane*
>   *Amang the heather."*

"Dear" and "auld" were the words that R.L.S. evoked in excuse for writing in the language; none knew better than he that his professional status and fame depended on good Southern Standard English. He foresaw: "The day draws near when this illustrious and malleable tongue shall be quite forgotten; and Burns's Ayrshire, and Dr [George]

38

MacDonald's Aberdeen-awa', and Scott's brave, metropolitan utterance will be all equally the ghosts of speech."

What he did not foresee was that some forty years later there would be yet another spirited revival spearheaded by Hugh MacDiarmid, a man who, when he returned from the Great War of 1914-18, was cultivating an English style just as sedulously as R.L.S., and turning out several more than promising lyrics in the Southern Standard version of the language.

It is naturally easier to understand why a few gifted Highlanders should doggedly persist in writing in Gaelic, which is a distinct language representing a recognisable ethnic group, than that Lowland Scots, whose *public* language for generations has been English, should write in what is, after all, a *dialect* of English, or at best a "vatting" of selected words and idioms from a national group of dialects. We called it "Inglis" until Gavin Douglas, at the beginning of the sixteenth century, taught us to call it "Scots." (The word "Lallans," meaning "Lowlands," occurred only rarely until Douglas Young took the cue from Edwin Muir that "Scots" should more properly refer to Gaelic: Sir James Wilson, in his monumental field studies of Lallans in this century, called it plainly "Lowland Scotch"). What we now call "English" was distinguished by Gavin Douglas as "Suthron" (Southern).

Until James VI of Scotland became James I of England in 1603, there was no doubt of what language Scottish litterateurs ought to use. James himself wrote Lallans poetry until he ascended the Westminster Throne. But soon after the Union of Crowns, William Drummond of Hawthornden, who must have habitually spoken Lallans like any other Lothian or Border laird, was writing with some distinction in Southern Standard. This was also the medium in which James Graham, Marquis of Montrose, wrote his moving prayer on the eve of his execution in 1650. So, by midway through the seventeenth century, English had become established as a literary language in Scotland, though it was well into the next century before even educated Scots acquired an accent that could be understood in the South.

English obtained a great boost in Scotland—first from the King James Bible, which we took to our hearts, and which made Southern Standard the language for worship and theological discussion; and secondly from the Union of Parliaments in 1707 which made it necessary for politically ambitious Scots to learn to speak to be understood, and not ridiculed, at Westminster. But the great store of anonymous ballads, and folksong generally, kept Lallans alive, even in the literary field, and made possible

39

the revival of Lallans poetry begun by Robert Sempill of Beltrees in the seventeenth century and pursued in the eighteenth by Allan Ramsay and Robert Fergusson, both inspirers of Robert Burns.

By Burns's day, Lallans was no longer spoken in public debate or regarded with favour in "polite society." Its constant use had already become the mark of the rustic or of the urban worker. Even today many of our poets write Scots class-consciously as well as to express a national-istic enthusiasm, or they tend to think of it as a medium for rustic themes (which some stigmatise as "kailyard"). The fact that Burns was believed to be "working-class" (he was really a market gardener's son, working in a family business, albeit a poor one, and later a farmer in his own right, and eventually a Civil Servant) encouraged many workers in his wake to use Lallans as their natural medium of self-expression and class feeling. It was, after all, the language of that classic of social-satiric poetry, *The Twa Dogs.*

On the other hand, it was county society, and often the ladies, who, inspired mainly by folksong refined for the drawing room, kept the banner of the Lowland tongue flying romantically into the early nine-teenth century. Jean Elliot, who wrote the Lallans version of "The Flowers of the Forest," and Lady Nairne, author of "Caller Herrin'" and "The Land o' the Leal," are cases in point, and their successors in our own era were Violet Jacob, Marion Angus and Helen B. Cruickshank. Most of them have come from the North-East, where middle-class use of Lallans, or as they call it, "the Doric," has persisted rather more than in the Industrial Belt, where dialect tends to be regarded as very plebeian.

In the modern scene, many of our Lallans practitioners have been university men, like Robert Fergusson and R.L.S. Such are Tom and Alexander Scott, Robert Garioch and J. K. Annand, all of whom, how-ever, had a genuine Lallans background in boyhood, and can check their literary usages against their recollections of spoken Scots. Douglas Young and Sydney Goodsir Smith were both men with overseas back-grounds who took up the study of the language on settling in their ancestral country, and both used it in idiosyncratic fashion. MacDiarmid deliberate-ly expanded his vocabulary well beyond the limits of his native Langholm speech, and Scots poets as a rule have not confined themselves to one local dialect.

This is true even of Robert Burns and Charles Murray, both of whom wrote in a generalised Lallans rather than in "Ayrshire" or "Gairie." Burns modelled his language on that of Robert Fergusson, an Edinburgh man with Fife and North-Eastern connections, who was also a student of traditional Scottish literary usages, so it is a mistake to assume that Burns was writing in the Ayrshire dialect, though the bias was naturally West Coast.

There is much to be said for Dr Tom Scott's argument that the word "Lallans" should be dropped in favour of Gavin Douglas's "Scots," as it tends to add to the confused prejudice that most of our modern Scottish writing is "synthetic" in a derogatory sense. Some of the extravagances of "synthetic Scots" as a cult have been satirised in Forbes Macgregor's *The Gowks o' Mowdieknowes*, and other "squibs," but most of our recognised Lallans poets are writing essentially in the language of Fergusson and Burns and, in prose, of Sir Walter Scott's *Wandering Willie's Tale* and Stevenson's *Thrawn Janet* and *Tod Lapraik*.

At the same time some of our best Scottish poets have stuck to the Drummond of Hawthornden tradition and to the use of the Queen's English. These include Norman MacCaig, Maurice Lindsay (who wrote a few poems in Lallans) and Liz Lochhead.

One wonders if either Robert Burns or Hugh MacDiarmid would have made such a mark in the world if they had confined themselves to English? Both were capable of it, but wrote their best works in Lallans, and could hardly have won more international renown if they had abandoned it. They might have developed, as Lewis Grassic Gibbon did, a manner of writing in a kind of Scots-English, with a distinctive lilt which could have preserved their national identity without unduly burdening the reader. Strangely enough, much of Burns is in English, and yet it is his Lallans passages which stick in the mind.

Many of us will continue to write in Lallans because we feel it expresses ourselves best. We follow Mallarmé's dictum that the duty of the poet is to "give a purer sense to the words of the tribe."

Gaelic in Print

FRANK THOMPSON

GAELIC was once the original tongue of the Kingdom of the Scots. It survived the saxonisation of Scotland by Malcolm Canmore's queen, St Margaret, to the extent that it was still on the tongue and lips of half the population of Scotland about the time of the Union of the Crowns in 1603. Then followed a tragic decline with an active government policy of extinction, hastened by acts of what can be truly called genocide. Still the language survived, though the Gaelic-speaking areas receded like an ageing hairline until at the present time when the domains of the language are effectively those of the north-western coastal areas of Scotland and in the Western Isles.

The first-ever book to be printed in Gaelic appeared in 1567. This was a translation of John Knox's Book of Common Order, to be followed, during the next 200 years, by a small number of works, mostly of a religious nature. One significant work was, however, a collection of poetry (Leith, 1751) by Alasdair Domnullach (Mac Mhaighstir Alasdair), innocently entitled *The New Gaelic Songster*, but containing poems of a political nature, which heaped invective on the reigning House of Hanover and its supporters. Thus earning the displeasure of the Government, MacDonald was pursued. But he escaped prosecution and the unsold copies of his work were siezed and burnt by the common hangman in Edinburgh's market place in 1752.

Until the beginning of the 19th century, publishing and writing in Gaelic was confined to ecclesiastical works and poetry. Then, in the early years of the 19th century, both writing and publishing in the language blossomed, as the following rounded-off figures show: 1830-40, 110 titles; 1840-50, 170; 1850-60, 120; 1860-70, 140; 1870-80, 170; 1880-90, 100; 1890-1900, 100. Then followed a decline.

The main reason suggested for the increased activity in the field of Gaelic literature is that Gaelic had become the language of a popular Church, which was also the medium of a popular educational movement; the latter, in its turn, created a popular literacy within the Highlands and the Hebrides. In addition, Gaelic spread into the areas in which, in its past history, it had held cultural and numerical supremacy: in the central belt of Scotland. This incursion into former areas was the direct result of the Clearances and the massive migration of Gaelic-speakers from their homelands. Arriving in urbanised areas, they quickly adapted to their new environment, and took on the trappings and facilities of city-dwellers, to use these to nurture their cultural norms: organising societies, Gaelic schools, classes for "improvement" and making full use of printing presses.

Gaelic publishing houses were established in Glasgow, Edinburgh, Stirling, and publishing societies also came into existence. Magazines and newspapers were also published in Gaelic, or contained a significant element in each issue in the language. Gaelic in fact became the language of the pulpit and religious literature, the medium of popular education, a secular press and of popular journalism.

After the first World War the Highland region went into a serious depression; indeed, it would not be far wrong to say that the region of the Highlands and Islands of Scotland was, for nearly three decades, the British equivalent of the deep American South populated by "poor white trash," though in the Highland context, the "trash" were Gaelic-speakers. The Hebrides in particular were subjected to visits by writers who sought "quaintness and whimsy" and refused to look behind the long-standing folklore and tradition of the region to see and write about the real reasons for social and economic deprivation.

At the present time Gaelic writing and publishing can be said to be in a reasonable state, but falls far below the standard of output one might expect from a linguistic community of 90,000 Gaelic speakers— particularly when one compares the publishing activity in other linguistic-minority communities (*e.g.* the Rhaeto-Romansh in Switzerland) in Europe with far less than 90,000 speakers, yet who manage, with subsidy, to support their writers and publishers. Another point which must be made is that it can be questioned whether the present Gaelic literary output is on the right lines to becoming a literature in its own right with international recognition (there is of course a vigorous "sub-literature" fostered by song, story and "village" verse which can offer a useful base for status but which falls rather short of the norms required by a developing literature to raise or enhance writing to the level of international acceptance).

If one takes numbers into account, the state of both writing and publishing looks good. In a recent *Catalogue of Gaelic Books in Print*, issued by the Gaelic Books Council in 1975, nearly 200 titles are available at the present time to the buyer of Gaelic reading material. However, if one looks closer, it will be found that many titles in the catalogue relate to material which cannot claim to be contributing anything significant to the image of "literature." A brief analysis shows: Vocabulary, 10; Textbooks, 18; Children's books, 17; Poetry, 35; Fiction, 12 collections of short stories and 3 novels; Biography, 3; Essays, 6; Collected writings, 2; Drama, 44.

Of these figures, two domains of writing are significant: poetry and fiction. The heavy emphasis on poetry writing reflects a long-standing tradition that this medium is the route to "literature;" indeed the heights to which this form of writing has attained places Gaelic poetry alongside the best of similar work by any writer in any minority- or majority-linguistic culture. Some of the work is truly international literature. The pity is that "international literati" are unaware of the levels achieved in Gaelic poetry because it has not been available through translations into majority-culture languages such as English and French. Some poetry, particularly that of Sorley Maclean, has had recent exposure in English translations which has resulted in an enhancement of Maclean's stature among European poets. However, while the literature of a culture stays locked away in its own language (as was once the work of internationally-known writers in Germany, Italy, Norway, Denmark and France), its claim to belong to world literature cannot be put to the critical test of assessment. It can perhaps be said that the expression of thought through the medium of poetry is a higher achievement than through prose, because of the severe restraints which this form of writing places on the poet. Others might argue that prose must also play a significant part in the development of the literature of any linguistic-minority culture.

Looking at the fiction titles in print, the emphasis is on the short story— yet another reflection of the traditional form of expression. It might be unkind to suggest that the Celtic mind in Gaelic Scotland is incapable of sustaining the longer period of gestation required in the production of a novel; but novels have been written in Gaelic, though they are few and far between, and the scarcity reflects, not inability, but the idea that the novel is a new medium for personal expression and has yet to be tested as to its relevance, and even its desirability, in Gaelic literary culture. Even so, international recognition for the literature of other linguistic communities has come through translations into English and French. One could point to the recognition by the international literati of works produced in Welsh or Irish, mainly because if translations of these works read good in English, so the originals must be that much better. So far Scottish Gaelic has not had this facility to international recognition.

Who are the Gaelic writers? Such names as James Thomson (poet and essayist), John N. MacLeod (dramatist and essayist), Donald Lamont (essayist), Norman MacLeod (poet and prose-writer) are familiar, even if some are better known through the medium of the anthology (usually used in schools), than their individually published works, many of which are now out of print. But their work, still current today, is of a former generation and their contribution is well acknowledged as being more than significant at a time when Gaelic writing was regarded as being an area into which one made an occasional incursion, a deployment rather than a commitment to keep a cultural pot simmering if not boiling. However, some of the recent generation are still with us A poet like Sorley Maclean is familiar enough throughout Scotland today. Yet his first publication was a joint effort with Robert Garioch, the Lallans poet, in which both Gaelic and Lowland Scots appeared cheek by jowl with no uneasiness . . . as they have done in the past decade with increasing frequency.

Maclean's contribution to *17 Poems for Sixpence* (a title perhaps reflecting the need for a wide market by placing the need to read before making money, as Joyce did with his *Poems Pennyeach*) was four numbered poems from the sequence "Dain do Eimhir," later to be published in 1943 by William MacLellan of Glasgow. It says much for Maclean's contribution to the standing and enhancement of Gaelic writing that his high reputation rests on this one published collection, *Dàin do Eimhir agus Dàin Eile*.

George Campbell Hay has used verse to wrench Gaelic into the horrors of the present, as witness his poem "Bisearta" (the burning of Bizerta in World War II). Donald MacAulay, of Lewis, now working in Aberdeen University, Iain Crichton Smith, also of Lewis and teaching in Oban, and Derick Thomson, of Glasgow University, are poets of a newer generation who have based their development on the literary inheritance left to them by their writing forebears and built up new facets of poetry, trying and testing language, metre, meanings, rhythms inherent in Gaelic, and exposing Gaelic to all the agencies for potential fragmentation, while assessing the results of their experimentation to make the language stronger and more able to cope with contemporary literary norms. That they have to a large extent succeeded is a tribute both to themselves, for the courage of their testing techniques (for if Gaelic had failed, both it and the poets would have suffered irreparable damage), and their commitment to the language.

Other poets such as Donald J. MacDonald, South Uist, Murdo MacFarlane, Lewis, Angus Campbell, Lewis and Donald Macintyre, South Uist, have tended to lean more heavily on traditional modes of poetic expression and thought, though their work is no less relevant in a contemporary context for that.

In fiction-writing, the emphasis has been on the short story, which has been subjected to much experimentation. Writers include Iain Crichton Smith, John Murray, Finlay J. MacDonald, Eilidh Watt, Norman Macdonald, Colin MacKenzie, John MacLeod, Mary MacLean; each has contributed their own brand of literary wine to the proceedings. The attraction, indeed the relevance, of the novel, has yet to appeal to these writers, though Smith and MacKenzie are among the few writers who have tackled the medium; indeed Smith has written a number of widely-accepted novels in English, each of which would have found a place, if not a market, in Gaelic. One might venture to say that the work of Smith, in English, both in poetry and prose, has made those whom I have termed the "international literati" to recognise that Smith is a window on the Gaelic world which exposes a minority-language community to close scrutiny and shows that there are literary gems awaiting translation, which process would allow Gaelic writers to take their place alongside their Celtic brethren from Eire, Wales and Brittany.

Last but hardly least come the Gaelic publishers. In the classified catalogue of *Gaelic Books in Print*, mentioned earlier, no fewer than forty names of publishers and distributors are given. At first sight this might indicate that publishers are falling over themselves to publish Gaelic writers. The opposite is the case. Of the forty publishers and distributors, only two names provide the main channels through which Gaelic writing can appear before the public: Gairm Publications, Glasgow, and Club Leabhar, Inverness.

The former started as *Gairm* magazine, founded by Derick Thomson and Finlay J. MacDonald, both from the Western Isles. The magazine, which has now been appearing regularly, four times each year, for over twenty years, has provided a much-needed platform for writers. Indeed, had it not been for *Gairm*, much of the excellent Gaelic writing of the present time would be still in an embryo experimental stage. Later the magazine extended its interests into publishing and the present set-up of Gairm Publications, which publishes in Gaelic only, is an all-aspect publishing concern, having a retail sales outlet in Glasgow, deals with mail order and operates with full- and part-time staff. The concern is in an advatageous position for advertising publications in Gaelic of all kinds.

Club Leabhar Limited (the Highland Book Club), started off as an investigating Committee of the Northern Regional Council of An Comunn Gaidhealach (the Highland Association) in 1966. After two years, the Committee dissolved itself and, in 1968, emerged as Club Leabhar Limited, a Company registered in Edinburgh with a limited capital of £100; it exists to publish books in Gaelic, books in English on subjects of Highland interest, and books by Highland authors choosing to write in English. Publishing operations began in 1969 and to date some 40 titles have appeared, many now out of print, of which more than half are in Gaelic or are bilingual.

The English-title productions of the Club are used to generate a profit (from their larger sales potential) so that the Gaelic publishing side of the operation can be subsidised. The Club is supported by about 500 members, who receive their choice of the Club's titles on discount and who make the difference between make and break in any one of the Club's editions.

It remains only to mention one of the most significant bodies to appear in the history of Gaelic writing and publishing: the Gaelic Books Council. The Council was established in 1968 to stimulate both Gaelic writing and publishing. The Council awards grants to publishers on the publication of approved Gaelic books. The sum of any grant allows the publisher to produce a work, either at a price amenable to the Gaelic market, or to enhance the production standards of a work. Writers are also offered cash rewards for their output. Recent developments in the Council's operations have included book-design schemes and commissions to writers for Gaelic work: factual, fiction and children's books.

For the first time in many decades it is now possible for a Gaelic author to write and receive some cash award for his effort. However, the rewards are pitifully small when compared with those available to writers in Eire and in Wales. For instance prizes running to three and four figures have been offered in the Oireachtas in Eire for literary competitions, while the National Mod in Scotland offers a paltry £75 for a full-length novel. Even so, the emergence of a corpus of Gaelic literature, though it varies considerably in quality, during the past decade has been a big step forward into a future which is as yet uncertain but which offers real potential for development and enhanced status of writers in the Gaelic-speaking community.

Gaelic publishing and writing are still fields where commitment to the culture is essential, without a beady eye to rewards offered to similar operators in minority- and majority-language cultures. To any writer an appreciative and critical audience is necessary for his further development and a continuing assessment of his worth; this recognition is, in a spiritual context, worth more than cash. For the publisher, because most publishing in Gaelic is carried on with varying degrees of financial loss or small profit margins, the rewards lie in the satisfaction of ensuring that the task of providing a medium for the writer to reach his or her audience is maintained. Both writer and publisher have an extremely close relationship of a kind which does not exist between large English publishing houses and their authors, where a writer is too often regarded as being a unit of commercial potential to the publisher. In the Gaelic field, both writer and publisher are integral elements in a combined operation, and both aim at the maintenance and enhancement of the language as a medium for cultural expression.

(For a full list of Gaelic books in print, obtain the Catalogue *Leabhraichean Gaidhlig*, price 25p, from the Gaelic Books Council, Department of Celtic, Glasgow University, Glasgow).

Writers and the Theatre

ALLEN WRIGHT

THE programme for the 30th Edinburgh Festival was devoid of Scottish drama but more than twenty works by Scottish writers were performed on the Fringe. There has never been a greater demonstration of the range of Scotland's play-writing talents and yet it passed virtually unnoticed by the London critics covering the Festival and Fringe. If such a wealth of native creativity were to be found at the Dublin Theatre Festival, the critics would probably remark on Ireland's good fortune to be so richly blessed with dramatists. In Edinburgh, there is such a welter of theatrical activity during the Festival that the explorer can easily miss some of the best plays.

With the exception of James Bridie, who was represented by *The Anatomist*, all the Scottish playwrights contributing to the 1976 Fringe were in the land of the living. Anyone familiar with the repertory theatres' programmes throughout the years might be astonished to learn that Scotland had as many as a score of living playwrights. Indeed, there may be twice that number, for there were some notable absentees from the Fringe programme. If there is no shortage of playwrights, why should there be so few Scottish plays in general circulation? Only one or two are performed each season at Perth, Dundee, Pitlochry and the Lyceum Theatre, Edinburgh, and the Citizens' Theatre Company in Glasgow avoid them like the plague. A few years ago, theatre directors used to argue that Scottish plays did not attract audiences but that generalisation was demolished by the success of Bill Bryden's *Willie Rough*, Hector Macmillan's *The Sash*, John McGrath's *The Cheviot, The Stag, and the Black, Black Oil*, and a revival of Robert McLellan's *The Flouers o' Edinburgh*.

The popularity of these plays had interesting repercussions. Encouraged by the success of *Willie Rough*, Roddy MacMillan wrote *The Bevellers* which took advantage of the Lyceum Company's talent for robust realism, and Bryden wrote *Benny Lynch*. Macmillan's skills were nurtured at Dundee Rep by Stephen Macdonald who directed *The Rising* and *The Royal Visit*. On becoming director of the Royal Lyceum Company in Edinburgh, Macdonald immediately set out to revive *The Royal Visit*. McGrath wrote a string of plays in a similar vein to *The Cheviot* . . . and even if they were not all of that quality, they secured a large and enthusiastic following for the work of the 7:84 Company. McLellan's *Flouers o' Edinburgh* was so widely appreciated that there will surely be revivals of some of his other plays. His *Torwatletie* was presented on the Edinburgh Festival Fringe where one of Alexander Reid's plays, *The Warld's Wonder*, was also revived. The work of both these playwrights has been too long neglected. Reid's *Lass wi' a Muckle Mou'* is due for reappraisal. The late Robert Kemp is another playwright of the same generation whose accomplishments have been ignored by professional theatre companies in recent years. Revivals of *The Other Dear Charmer* at Pitlochry and of *Let Wives Tak Tent* at Dundee may have begun the process of reinstatement.

McLellan, Reid and Kemp all benefited enormously from working with Duncan Macrae who was a national theatre in himself. His death dealt the Scottish stage a very serious blow and while the older playwrights have been unable to find anyone to fill his shoes, the younger writers have been slow to learn the lesson: that playwrights can profit from partnership with an individual actor. The close association between James Bridie and Alistair Sim is probably the best example of collaboration between an author and interpreter. Few modern Scottish writers have established this kind of creative partnership. It might not be to the advantage of the author or the actor if they were to monopolise each other's services, but both Macrae and Sim showed what could be done. Possibly the only lasting partnership between an actor and author in Scotland today is that between Russell Hunter and W. Gordon Smith. *Jock* and *Knox* are two of the products of their combined skills.

On the strength of *The Sash*, Macmillan might have been expected to continue his association with Andrew Keir but no doubt they had their reasons for separating and the stage has been deprived of a potentially great partnership. Fulton Mackay, Tom Fleming, Roddy McMilan, Andrew Cruickshank and Rikki Fulton are some of the leading actors who might profit from regularly working with a particular dramatist and vice versa. Similarly, if Billy Connolly were to write another play, he would be wise to enlist the services of Bill Paterson who gave such a memorable performance in *An' Me Wi' a Bad Leg Tae*, and Donald Campbell would seem to bring out the best in Roy Hanlon who portrayed Andrew with such strength in *The Jesuit*. For that reason, one would expect Campbell to create a part for Hanlon in his next play. Such are

50

the exigencies of theatrical presentation however that it may not be as simple as it seems for authors to form alliances with actors. The latter may be otherwise engaged when the opportunity arises, and writers find that they have to deal with theatre directors rather than the people who will actually perform their plays.

Administratively, it is more convenient for playwrights to be attached to companies rather than individuals. John McGrath is in the special situation of writing for his own company, whose personnel changes from time to time without altering the general character and commitment. Bill Bryden built up the company which performed his work but he was also in the privileged position of being director as well as author. Tom Gallacher has been associated with Pitlochry Festival Theatre for several years, becoming its playwright-in-residence, but his work seems to have suffered from inconsistency of casting. The Pitlochry company changes each season and each of his plays has had a fresh cast, so that no actors have become steeped in the Gallacher style. He needs to find actors who can adjust themselves to his wavelength and bring out the full significance of his plays.

One comes across many instances of directors regularly collaborating with certain playwrights. When Max Stafford-Clark was at the Traverse Theatre, he seemed to complement Stanley Eveling's plays in a way which few other directors have been able to achieve. Joan Knight has demonstrated her enthusiasm and respect for William Watson's plays at Perth and Pitlochry and Stephen Macdonald has formed a rewarding partnership with Hector Macmillan. Macdonald also helped to restore Stewart Conn's confidence in his own play-writing ability by mounting a production of *The Aquarium* at Dundee where it worked much more successfully that it had done previously in Edinburgh. Macdonald also revived one of Conn's earliest works *I Didn't Always Live Here*.

Most playwrights in Scotland are, however, unattached to any director or company of actors. Some of them expect recognition and become frustrated, but they might have more success if they approached directors and actors who appeared to be working towards the same goal as themselves. Among the disappointed playwrights, there is a tendency to deplore the policies of various theatre directors. It would be more sensible to exploit the openings which do exist. There is no sense in sending realistic working-class drama to the Citizens' Theatre, Glasgow, when it is obviously that theatre's policy to present elaborately stylised plays. It would be equally futile to expect Pitlochry Festival Theatre to accept a stark piece about sexual perversions, or the Traverse to present a cosy drawing-room comedy. The trouble with many aspiring play-wrights is that they genuinely believe they are God's gift to the stage, and not even unfavourable reviews and indifferent audiences can disabuse them of this idea. I am not suggesting that modesty will advance their careers. Self-projection is essential in the hurly-burly of the Theatre, but playwrights should make it their business to cultivate the acquaintance of directors and actors and find out what they want and what they think the public are seeking.

Writers should go to the theatre more often to learn from the achievements and mistakes of their colleagues. It may be galling to watch some of the awful new plays which do gain acceptance, but one may gradually discern which directors and actors are best equipped to present one's own plays.

Small theatres like the Traverse, and the Lyceum's studio offer the best opportunity for new work and the productions need not be short-lived. One of the most heartening developments of recent times has been the way in which successful productions from the Traverse have gone out on tour and have been revived on the Edinburgh Festival Fringe. The old system of treating plays as disposable objects which were dumped after two weeks is, fortunately, changing. If a production appears to merit a wider audience, then some effort is made to arrange a tour. There are community centres throughout the country waiting to receive small-scale productions like those of the 7:84 Company, Ayrshire's Borderline Company, and the Traverse. On a larger scale, there are excellent modern theatres in Inverness and Stirling which can take touring productions from the Lyceum, Perth and Pitlochry. The contemporary playwright can reach far more people in Scotland than Bridie and Barrie could in the days when professional theatre was confined to the large centres of population. The great danger is that limited funds will make theatre companies play safe with established works instead of taking the risk of presenting new Scottish plays.

Writing for Radio and Television

STEPHEN MULRINE

To COMPARE writing for the broadcast media, with the more ancient forms of literature, always suggests to me the same kind of prickly dialogue between "design" and "fine art," which not infrequently enlivens staff meetings at the art college where I work. Designers have a client, a brief, a deadline. Artists have a vision. And indeed, from a lay standpoint the split seems deceptively clear, even in terms of individual psychology— the design outlook, artistic temperament. It is of course, in any complete sense, an illusion. Designers of wildly creative ability role-play the professional hack, Mammon-worship; artists of microscopic talent saw off ears with the best. But just as good design transcends the limitations of any brief, so no creative artist can properly develop without some external pressure.

All this is relevant to the writer in a variety of ways. For a start, the kind of prestige which adheres to "fine art" has an obvious parallel in that enjoyed by the more traditional literary forms; to instance, I recently had a polite enquiry from a magazine editor, as to whether I was still writing these days. It was kindly meant, of course, but I must confess to an absurd feeling of guilt at having had to reply no, I had *not* written any new poems. The experience, I am told, is not uncommon. Poetry apart, the printed word generally cuts far more ice than any event on television or radio, at least among one's literary peers, and writers' directories, for example (though not this one), usually list publications only. What is a more serious inequality in the prestige stakes is the comparative lack of critical attention paid to the broadcast media. To take a concrete example, Peter McDougall's *Just Another Saturday* got a number of deservedly ecstatic reviews, but they were as nothing compared with the heavy critical artillery turned upon Bill Bryden's *Willie Rough*, nowhere near as good a play, but written for the prestige medium of the Lyceum stage. As it happens, at the time of writing, *Willie Rough* has just been networked as a teleplay, and the difference in critical comment now and then is worth remarking. Then, it was a seminal event in Scottish drama, etc., now, it is notable for Fulton Mackay's albeit marvellous performance. And therein lies the nub—television is about actors, real writers make it in the theatre. An extended comparison between theatre and television reviewing in our quality newspapers will disclose the same bias—critics for the stage, journalists for the box. The amount of cover of any description given to radio writing, moreover, is negligible. In this connection, the certainty of a sizeable audience has to compensate the writer for a lack of professional notice—as a good poster design makes its impact in the street, and not in the gallery.

In terms of the work itself, of course, that very audience can have a depressant effect on creativity. The familiar and repeatable are always a temptation, even if not an actual imposition upon the media writer; the uncompromising commitment of the gallery filters out to the street but sparingly, and perhaps too slowly for our more explosive talents. Compromise is in artistic bad odour these days, but really it is an essential element in any work for the mass audience, and, I would argue, potentially as much a stimulus as a limitation. Even the "purest" media creation, the one-off original teleplay, has a rigidly-timed slot, and because of the economics of the business, quite possibly no more than four characters, two studio interiors, and-if-you-want-exterior-film-no-lip-sync-sound-please. It is a question of temperament, I suppose, but some writers undoubtedly bridle at such things. For those who do not, however, radio and television offer the very real satisfaction of operating as a key member of a team, an activity which goes far beyond the provision of a text for "them" to loose their technology upon.

Most of the opportunities for the writer in the broadcast media are in fact commissioned, on the basis of proven ability to work in this fashion, but the classic mode of entry is still the unsolicited one-off playscript, and probably a radio play at that. At the time of writing, Radio Scotland is in mid-flow of a series of six new plays by Scottish writers. And while the radio output is sadly under-publicised, it is no exaggeration to say that if the work is good enough, by a fairly catholic definition that embraces the quality potboiler as well as "Radio 3," then a slot will be found for it, if necessary by "opting out" of one of the network drama placings. This is a distinct advantage, to the writer, of the peculiar regional set-up of Scottish broadcasting, though, drama excepted, it has in the past come under deserved attack for tending to encourage parochialism. Also, uniquely in Scotland, Edinburgh's Radio Forth maintains a commitment to drama production; the attempt has been made, in commercial radio elsewhere in the U.K., to employ actors in scripted drama, but one suspects more in order to pay some sort of lip-service to the franchise application, than to overturn the needle-time, phone-in pattern. Radio Forth, to their credit, have doubled their drama output, in their second year of existence. Radio Clyde, please copy.

How long Scottish radio can continue to offer this kind of outlet for the writer is anybody's guess, but if radio drama should go under the loss would be catastrophic. The term "nursery slopes" is altogether too patronising for a medium that, used effectively, is the most evocative of any, but it is quite true that radio's off-centre, Cinderella status does allow producers to take chances with new writers, to let them develop through the invaluable experience of hearing their work performed, in a way that neither television nor the live theatre could afford to. Performance is an absolute necessity for the dramatist, and I should think that, given the hypothetical stack of unproduced plays in a locked drawer, the last would be as bad, or as good as the first. Playwriting is an acquired skill, and radio is the perfect medium, whether for learning the basics, or pushing out to the limits. Writers and actors both have a soft spot for radio, in my experience, that is not mere nostalgic sentiment. The fact is that radio production, without all the awe-inspiring hardware of TV, demonstrably cherishes the writer's script, every syllable of it; and it is a truism that the radio microphone sorts out sheep from goats among actors. The camera can create a performance where none exists, but a good radio actor needs a high degree of intelligence, as well as technique, to bring his character to life.

If I have said almost as much about the actor, and the producer, as the writer in broadcasting, it is because although the relationship of each to the other is well enough defined in theory, it is in practice often more complex—a creative symbiosis. Instead of the private Muse of poetry, imagine the radio writer at work, on an idea furnished by a producer, with an actor's familiar voice supplying the speech rhythms in his mind's ear. Paradoxically, it can be a stimulus to creativity, not a hindrance.

The writer who sees all these things as limitations is unlikely to be successful in broadcasting, and certainly not in educational broadcasting, which in Scotland at any rate still offers the widest range of TV outlets for the writer. As with radio, these tend to be under-publicised, but in the case of educational TV there is no market whatever for the unsolicited script. To begin with, the specialised nature of the programmes, in terms of age-group, educational function, and so on, precludes the use of anything but commissioned material. And of necessity, since the year's programming is committed to print, in teachers' notes, for example, well in advance of transmission, the writer's ability to deliver the goods to a tight schedule, is at a premium. Almost equally prized is the writer's readiness to bring his vision into line with that of the producer, director, and if need be the Schools Broadcasting Council—though (saving the latter body), that bald statement of the political realities should not obscure, in my own experience, some very enjoyable working relationships. Educational broadcasting in fact offers a great variety of work, from the documentary careers and guidance kind of programme, to freewheeling short plays, limited only by the known age of the audience. The same department's Further Education output, generally in an evening placing, has no such restriction, and the fact that the main outline of any documentary series—on archaeology, architecture, contemporary literature, criminology, or whatever—will come from the producer, simply means that the writer fortunate enough to land an F.E. commission starts with all the freedom he is likely to want; the rest is budget, and consultation, fining the ideas down, to treatment, to drafts, to the finished script. Some writers revel in the whole process, exposing the third or fourth "final" draft to yet another brainstorming, the eleventh-hour panic 'phone-call to cut a minute-and-a-half out, we're over-running, for Godssakes—a minute-and-a-half, but that's two hundred *words*! That may not be compatible with art, but most of our leading dramatists have worked for "Schools"—including Cecil Taylor, Tom Gallacher, Peter McDougall, and Hector MacMillan. Indeed, the latest recruit to the fold is Alasdair MacLean, with no form as anything but one of the most exciting poets to emerge at the "prestige" end of Scottish literature in recent years. The message is obvious enough, at least to the broadcasting professionals, that the best creative writing, and craftsmanship, of the kind their livelihoods depend upon, go hand in glove.

A fair number of adults watch daytime Schools programmes, not that one would expect critics, outside the pages of the *Times Ed. Supp.*, to notice them. But the lack of serious criticism of radio and TV plays, as compared with stage plays, is quite unjustifiable, the more so when they are written by the same people. A new stage-play by Cecil Taylor, for example, is an *event*; at the time of writing, a new radio play by the same author has raised not a ripple. And who would believe that the country's best theatre critic does not possess a television set, wouldn't have one in the house?

Still, there are signs of better days ahead. Apart from taking the Italia Prize, in international competition, Peter McDougall's *Just Another Saturday* rated mention as the best *networked* play in several national press reviews of the year's TV; and within this current month, *two* Plays for Today in succession have been Scottish. It matters little that *Clay, Smeddum, and Greenden* was a literary adaptation, and not Bill Craig's original work; it was done impressively well, and gained us another foothold on the network. In the long run, that is where the battle has to be won, and BBC Scotland's Controller Alistair Hetherington sees it as a major policy aim. Drama is a labour-intensive art-form in any medium, and commitment and vision, unhappily, can't be coined to finance production. The obvious answer, particularly in television, is not to opt out, in the interests of preserving our regional identity—the fallacy of that argument is exposed regularly by Light Entertainment's swirling kilts—but to opt *in* to the network, to make our culture, and individuality, and speech, as much part of the Home Counties' consciousness as the once-despised North of England now is, and in the same way—to put the tale over by the strength of the telling.

As everyone recognises, Scotland is enjoying something of a theatrical renaissance at the present time—no obvious giants, but most of the necessary conditions for growth, undeniably. For television, the potential is there, if the placings can be won.

Money makes money; quality productions of good plays make more of the same possible. It is certainly a surprise to me, and a note of cautious optimism on which to end, that in a deepening gloom of retrenchments and economies in broadcasting, a chink of light *is* opening up—for the writer, because of the writer.

Scottish Broadcasting Facilities

Contrary to popular belief both radio and television welcome submission of new works suitable for broadcasting, and are happy to encourage and develop new writers adaptable to the needs and disciplines of the medium. Producers are well aware that the future strength of broadcast drama depends on the constant discovery of fresh talents.

Radio plays for the BBC should be submitted to the Radio Drama Department, Broadcasting House, 5 Queen Street, Edinburgh 2; short stories and talks to the Senior Producer, Talks and Features, Radio, at the same address.

Plays of 30, 45 and 55 minutes, and full-length original work or dramatisation of novels and adaptation of stage plays of 75 and 90 minutes are acceptable for Radio Scotland and for submission to Radio 4. Durations are more flexible for Radio 3.

For television, plays and adaptations should be submitted to the TV Drama Department, Broadcasting House, Queen Margaret Drive, Glasgow G12 8DG. A leaflet is available on BBC-TV Script Requirements.

The other broadcasting companies in Scotland which also use original work and adaptations are:

Scottish Television. The Script Editor, Cowcaddens, Glasgow G2 3PR.

Grampian Television. Queen's Avenue, Aberdeen.

Radio Clyde. 16 Fitzroy Place, Glasgow G.3.

Radio Forth. Forth House, Forth Street, Edinburgh 1.

The Scottish Stage

Ironically, the collapse of the commercial theatre in Scotland has greatly stimulated dramatic enterprise. Civic and repertory theatres and travelling companies, with financial support from the Scottish Arts Council, local authorities and other sources, are having a stimulating influence on audiences throughout the country. For box-office reasons plays that are established successes or have a wide range of appeal inevitably occupy a considerable part of the repertory, but a number of companies, notably the Traverse and the Royal Lyceum in Edinburgh, do present new plays and actively encourage the work of Scottish writers. Production companies include the following:

Dundee Repertory Theatre

Edinburgh: Traverse Theatre, 112 West Bow.

                 Royal Lyceum Theatre, Grindlay Street.

                 7:84 Company, 58 Queen Street.

Glasgow: Citizens' Theatre, 119 Gorbals Street.

              Strathclyde Theatre Group, Strathclyde University.

Irvine: Borderline Theatre Company, Barnett House, Harbour Street.

Mull Little Theatre, Dervaig, Isle of Mull.

Ochtertyre Theatre, Crieff.

Perth Repertory, Perth Theatre.

Pitlochry Festival Theatre, Pitlochry.

St Andrews: Byre Theatre.

Promoting Literature

THE SCOTTISH ARTS COUNCIL

THE SCOTTISH ARTS COUNCIL is the government's main agency for the distribution of public funds in support of the Arts in Scotland. It is composed of twenty-two members appointed by the Arts Council of Great Britain with the approval of the Secretary of State for Scotland, and it shares the same objectives as the ACGB—

1. to develop and improve the knowledge, understanding and practice of the arts
2. to increase the accessibility of the arts to the public throughout Great Britain, and
3. to advise and co-operate with government departments, local authorities and other bodies on any other matters concerned directly or indirectly with these objects.

Its primary purpose is to give financial assistance to artistic institutions (independent non-profit making organisations such as orchestras, opera and ballet companies, theatre, art galleries, arts centres and festivals) and also direct help to individual artists. It also surveys, plans and advises, and promotes exhibitions. Out of its allocation from the Government, £25 million in 1975-76, ACGB gave a block grant to the Scottish Arts Council (roughly 12%—£3 million in 1975-76) and to the Welsh Arts Council (roughly 8%—£2,050,000 in 1975-76).

The Council spends some 3% (£91,000 in 1975-76) on literature activities in Scotland. Roughly a quarter of this money is allocated to direct help to writers in Scotland. Bursaries worth £750-£2000 are awarded each year to writers to enable them to concentrate on their work or to finish particular projects; Book Awards worth £400 each are awarded to the authors of books of literary merit and a number of fellowships are maintained in association with various universities and local authorities (Universities of Dundee and Glasgow, Aberdeen Art Gallery, Lothian Region and Sabhal Mor Ostaig, Skye). As part of its help to writers, the Council with the help of Glenrothes Development Corporation established a Writers' House on the Balbirnie Estate in Markinch. The cottage offers peace and quiet to writers who want to finish projects.

The Council also gives publication assistance to eight literary magazines. This enables the magazines to be professionally published, to appear regularly and to pay contributors' fees. The magazines have a co-operative sales organisation, the Scottish Association of Magazine Publishers (SCAMP), which promotes and sells the publications throughout Scotland. SCAMP is supported by the Scottish Arts Council.

Publishers, too, may apply to the Council for financial assistance towards the costs of producing books of literary interest which involve a commercial risk. Grants of up to 40% of the production costs make these books more widely available as well as providing a guarantee against loss for the publisher. The recent initiative by the Scottish publishers to form a professional association, the Scottish General Publishers' Association, has resulted in the Council assisting the appearance of members of the Association at the Frankfurt and Montreal Book Fairs. Other publications assisted by the Council are the production of films on writers, and cassettes and long-playing gramophone records of poets reading their work.

Although the greater part of the Council's literature budget is spent on direct aid to writers and publishers, the Council has provided financial backing for initiatives which bring the writer into direct contact with the public. The most successful of these is Writers in Schools, a scheme which allows writers to be invited to give talks about their work in Scottish secondary schools. Poetry readings, Writers' Tours and Meet the Author sessions in various parts of Scotland are also given modest support.

The Council, as the national body for the arts in Scotland, maintains links with other countries and in recent years writers from America, Nigeria, Germany, Sweden, USSR and Israel have visited Scotland as the Council's guests to give talks and readings. As a memorial to the late Neil Gunn, the Council instituted the Neil Gunn Fellowship in 1973. The purpose of the fellowship is to honour distinguished novelists from other countries and to invite them to visit Scotland. The first two holders of the Fellowship were Heinrich Böll (1973, and Chinua Achebe (1975).

An annual exchange of Irish and Scots Gaelic-speaking poets and musicians has been maintained with the Comhdháil Náisiúnta na Gaeilge in Dublin since 1971. The Council also gives assistance to the publication of books in Gaelic by giving some financial support to the work of the Gaelic Books Council.

Further information about the Council's work may be obtained from the Literature Department, Scottish Arts Council, 19 Charlotte Square, Edinburgh EH2 4DF.

THE NATIONAL BOOK LEAGUE

THE NATIONAL BOOK LEAGUE is an independent, non-commercial organisation whose function is to promote books, reading and authors, and to provide information about all aspects of the book world to its members. The NBL Scottish Office (1121 Paisley Road West, Glasgow G52 1EQ) carries out all the activities of the NBL for its members in Scotland, including the distribution of booklists and bibliographies, and exhibitions of books on particular subjects. Because of the importance of forming the reading habit at an early age, much of its work is concerned with books and information for young people. The Scottish Office also takes a close interest in Scottish writers and books concerning Scotland, and among other booklists and exhibitions always includes some of particular Scottish interest in its annual programme. Among recent examples are a catalogue and exhibition of the work of *Scottish Small Presses*, a complete list of all books in print concerning the *Highlands and Islands of Scotland* and an annual exhibition *Scottish Writing Today*, which contains books over a wide range of subjects published during the past few years.

The NBL also operates a Readers' Information Service, to which any queries about books can be directed, and from which short reading lists of books currently in print can be obtained on any subject. Amongst other activities are the organisation of occasional discussions or conferences, and talks by authors.

INTERNATIONAL PEN SCOTTISH CENTRE

PEN (poets, publishers essayists, editors, novelists) is an international fellowship of writers with branches in some seventy countries throughout the world. Its members stand for the freedom of the written and spoken word and the free communication of writers, recognising no political barriers. Membership of Scottish PEN is open to any writer who has some published work to his credit. Regular meetings are held during the winter months, at which members discuss matters of common interest. Scottish PEN, in common with most other countries, contributes towards the expense of sending one or two members as delegates to meetings of International PEN, which are held usually twice a year in various countries. At these meetings problems concerning writers are discussed, particularly the cases of writers imprisoned for their beliefs.

The Hon. Secretary of PEN Scottish Centre is Miss Mary Baxter, 18 Crown Terrace, Glasgow G12 9ES.

THE SCOTTISH ASSOCIATION OF WRITERS

THE SCOTTISH ASSOCIATION OF WRITERS began in 1969, to promote the interchange of ideas and experiences of the members of Writers' Clubs in Scotland. At that time there were only five Writers' Clubs in Scotland —Glasgow (founded 1929) Edinburgh (1947) and Greenock, Aberdeen and the Highland Writers' Circle, all begun after the mid-nineteen sixties. These banded together in 1969 to form an association, and promote an annual Week-end School, since then held at Pitlochry.

Competitions (now nine in number) take place at the Annual Conference. These cover all forms of writing. Speakers and Adjudicators, well-known in their particular sphere of literature, are invited to attend. Among many other prizes is the Constable Trophy (gifted by Constable & Co., Publishers, London), presented each year for the best book submitted for competition. This was first offered in 1972. It has encouraged the emergence of new novelists. The Association has also encouraged Scottish writing in great variety, and many attending the Week-end School are now publishing more and more of their work, since marketing is one of the subjects dealt with at the School.

Since its inauguration in 1969, three more Writers' Clubs or Groups have been formed, and are now affiliated to the Association.

The Scottish Association is administered by a Committee of representatives drawn from all the Clubs and elected each year.

The Hon. Secretary is Mrs Ruby Turberville, 21 Belvidere Street, Aberdeen.

THE SOCIETY OF AUTHORS

Founded in 1884 to further the interests of authors and protect their rights, the Society of Authors advances the cause of writers by discussions with Government departments, broadcasting authorities, the Arts Council, publishers, etc. It also provides legal advice on taxation, contracts etc

The Hon. Secretary of the Scottish Committee is Miss Lavinia Derwent, 1 Great Western Terrace, Glasgow G12 0UP.

SCOTTISH SOCIETY OF PLAYWRIGHTS

Founded in 1973, the Scottish Society of Playwrights aims to promote the development and production of theatre-writing in Scotland and to act for playwrights in all matters affecting them.

The Society arranges seasons of plays and a "theatre workshop" for presenting "work in progress." It has instituted a publications service and submits scripts to production companies.

Miss Linda Haase, Administrator SCP, Third Eye Centre, 350 Sauchiehall Street, Glasgow.

ASSOCIATION FOR SCOTTISH LITERARY STUDIES

Formed to promote the study, teaching and writing of Scottish literature and to further the study of the languages of Scotland, the Association for Scottish Literary Studies holds conferences and residential schools, publishes volumes of edited texts, the *Scottish Literary Journal* and an occasional newsletter.

ASLS, Department of English, University of Aberdeen, Old Aberdeen AB9 2UB.

THE SCOTS LANGUAGE SOCIETY

Devoted to the study and encouragement of writing in Lowland Scots, the Scots Language Society holds conferences, discussions and competitions and publishes a magazine, *Lallans*, most of which is written in Scots.

Hon. Sec., David Angus, 122 Henderson Street, Bridge of Allan, Stirling.

THE GAELIC BOOKS COUNCIL

The Gaelic Books Council, supported by an annual grant of £8500 direct from the Scottish Education Department and £7000 in 1976-77 from the Scottish Arts Council, helps publishers produce a wide range of books through its production grants scheme. The Council also assists the promotion and distribution of these books through its book van which regularly tours the Western Islands and the Gaelic speaking areas of the mainland. The book van was bought and set up with grants from the Highlands and Islands Development Board and the Scottish Arts Council.

The Gaelic Books Council, Department of Celtic, University of Glasgow, Glasgow G12 8RZ.

CLUB LEABHAR

CLUB LEABHAR was formed in 1969 to offer Highland authors, and authors of Highland subjects, a publishing facility which would translate their works into print. For an annual subscription members may choose up to four books a year in either Gaelic or English. Books cover a broad range of interests, including poetry and fiction, Gaelic culture and works on the social and economic aspects of Highland life. Among authors published by Club Leabhar are Iain Crichton Smith, Neil Gunn, Lorn M. Macintyre, Norman Macdonald, Mary M. Maclean, Calum Maclean and Francis Thompson.

Club Leabhar Ltd., 31 Braeside Park, Balloch, Inverness IV1 2HJ.

Scottish Publishers

Akros Publications
14 Parklands Avenue, Penwortham, Preston, Lancashire PR1 0QL.
Though run from England, Akros is an entirely Scottish enterprise, conducted by Duncan Glen, which has made a notable contribution to the publication of Scottish literature and in particular to verse in Scots.

Albyn Press
2 Howe Street, Edinburgh EH3 6TD.
General literature, books of Scottish interest, cookery books.

An Comunn Gaidhealach
Abertarf House, Church Street, Inverness.
Est. 1891. Gaelic literature, informational handbooks, school taxts.

The Aquila Publishing Co., Ltd.
9 Scallamus, Breakish, Isle of Skye, IV42 8QB.
Est. 1968. Poetry, short stories, novels, literary criticism. Particularly interested in translations, American writing and work in other languages. Not in the narrow sense a "Scottish" publisher but willing to consider work by Scottish writers on Scottish literature.

John Bartholomew & Son Ltd.
Duncan Street, Edinburgh EH9 1TA.
World famous for maps and atlases. Also publish practical handbooks and illustrated works.

Blackie and Son Ltd.
Bishopbriggs, Glasgow G64 2NZ.
Scientific, technical and children's books.

William Blackwood and Sons Ltd.
32 Thistle Street, Edinburgh EH2 1HA.
Est. 1804. Biography, memoirs, history, higher education, professional works.

Caithness Books
Janet Street, Thurso.
Est. 1965. Local history, Scottish poetry, literary essays.

Canongate Publishing Ltd.
17 Jeffrey Street, Edinburgh EH1 1DR.
Fiction, biography, poetry, plays, children's books.

W. & R. Chambers Ltd.
11 Thistle Street, Edinburgh EH2 1DG.
Publishers of the famous *Chambers' Dictionary*, reference and educational works and books for children. Have recently instituted £1000 awards for work by Scottish authors.

Club Leabhar Ltd. (The Highland Book Club)
31 Braeside Park, Balloch, Inverness IV1 2HJ.

Est. 1968. Fiction, non-fiction, poetry and plays in Gaelic, English and bi-lingual. Highland subjects in English and Gaelic. Aims to promote the work of Highland based authors, in Gaelic or English.

William Collins, Sons & Co. Ltd.
144 Cathedral Street, Glasgow G4 0NB.

Est. 1880. Scotland's largest publisher. Fiction and almost every category of non-fiction, reference, educational and children's books. Fontana Paperbacks.

John Donald Publishers Ltd.
8 Mayfield Terrace, Edinburgh EH9 1SA.

History, art and general books of Scottish interest. Also the Scottish Reprint Library of facsimile reproductions.

Edinburgh University Press
22 George Square, Edinburgh.

Est. originally 1637—present Press 1948. Literature, science, economics, law, history, Scottish, Islamic.

Edinburgh University Student Publications Board
1 Buccleuch Place, Edinburgh WH8 9LW.

Political and social surveys.

Famedram Publishers Ltd.
School Road, Gartocharn, Alexandria, Dunbartonshire.

Popular handbooks, local interest, railways.

Gairm Publications
29 Waterloo Street, Glasgow G2.

Est. 1952, incorporating Alexander Maclaren and Son, 1875. Gaelic books including poetry, fiction, drama, biography, music, current affairs, manuals, dictionaries, text-books.

Paul Harris Publishing
25 London Street, Edinburgh EH3 6LY.

Fiction, biography, art, general.

Holmes McDougall Ltd.
Allander House, 137-141 Leith Walk, Edinburgh EH6 8NS.

General and educational.

Johnston and Bacon
Tanfield House, Tanfield Lane, Edinburgh EH3 5LL.

Maps, guides, books about Scotland and Ireland.

Lothlorien
118 Brankholm Brae, Hamilton, Lanarkshire.

Poetry, essays, works of philosophical, literary and Scottish interest, translations.

Macdonald Publishers (M. Macdonald, Edinburgh)
Edgefield Road, Loanhead, Midlothian EH20 9SY.

Mainly poetry and literary criticism.

Heatherbank Press
163 Mugdock Road, Milngavie, Dunbartonshire.

Mainly sociological works.

William Maclellan
104 Hill Street, Glasgow G3 6UA.
Art, poetry, folklore and general books of Scottish interest.

The Molendinar Press
73 Robertson Street, Glasgow G2.
Books of general Scottish interest, facsimile reprints.

Oliver and Boyd
Croythorn House, 23 Ravelston Terrace, Edinburgh EH4 3TJ.
Est. 1778, now a division of the Longman Group, London. Education and Scottish books.

Q Press
58 Queen Street, Edinburgh EH2 3NS.
Political, current affairs.

The Ramsay Head Press
36 North Castle Street, Edinburgh EH2 3BN.
Est. 1970. Biography, art, architecture, poetry, short stories, history, topography, reference. Aims to encourage creative work, irrespective of source.

Rainbow Books
171 Victoria Road, Aberdeen AB1 3ND.
Est. 1972. Poetry, Scottish fiction, material of local interest.

Scottish Academic Press Ltd.
33 Montgomery Street, Edinburgh WH7 5JX.
Est. 1969. General academic and scholarly works, literature, history, economics, social sciences, philosophy, natural history, mathematics.

The Standard Press (Montrose) Ltd.
66 High Street, Montrose, Angus.
Biography, history, topography and books of mainly Scottish interest.

Thuleprint Ltd.
Compass House, Sandwick, Shetland.
Est. 1973. Poetry, fiction, local topography and history, mostly relating to Shetland and Orkney.

Volturna Press
Mains of Kinmundy, Longside, Peterhead.
Religion, history, family memoirs and chronicles, books of Scottish and Irish interest.

Wilfion Books
12 Townhead Terrace, Paisley, Renfrewshire PA1 2AX.
Mainly poetry. A new publisher with "a distinctly international outlook."

Gordon Wright Publishing
55 Marchmont Road, Edinburgh EH9 1HT.
Biography, poetry and books of general Scottish interest.

Scottish authors whose work has a general appeal furth of Scotland appear in the lists of many English publishers who operate throughout the United Kingdom and the

English-speaking world. Among those who devote particular attention to books of Scottish interest are the following:

B. T. Batsford Ltd., 4 Fitzhardinge Street, London W1H 0AH. Topography, arts and crafts.

Carcanet Press, 330-332 Corn Exchange Building, Manchester M4 3BG. Poetry, literary criticism.

John Calder (Publishers) Ltd., 18 Brewer Street, London W1. Poetry, drama, fiction, general, the Scottish Library series.

Chatto and Windus and Hogarth Press, 40 William IV Street, London WC2. Fiction, poetry, general.

David and Charles Ltd., Brunel House, Forde Road, Newton Abbot, Devon. Art, architecture, crafts, topography, local history, transport, natural history.

Robert Hale & Co., Ltd., 45-47 Clerkenwell Green, London EC1R 0HT. Fiction, topography, arts, history, biography, general.

Hodder & Stoughton Ltd., St Paul's House, Paternoster Row, London EC4. Fiction, biography, general, children's.

Hamish Hamilton Ltd., 90 Great Russell Street, London WC1B 3PT. Fiction and non-fiction, children's.

Routledge and Kegan Paul, 76 Carter Lane, London EC4V 5EL. History, sociology, literature, the Scottish Series.

Scottish Literary Journals

Akros
14 Parklands Avenue, Penwortham, Preston, Lancashire PR1 0QL.
Editor, Duncan Glen. April, August, December. Mainly Scottish poetry and criticism of work by Scottish poets. Prose contributions, 2000-6000 words.

Blackwood's Magazine
32 Thistle Street, Edinburgh EH2 1HA.
Editor, David Fletcher. Est. 1817. Though less controversial than in its early years, *Blackwood's* continues to publish outstanding stories, poetry and articles by both new and distinguished writers.

Calgacus
Dormie, by Kyle of Lochalsh, Ross-shire.
Editor, Ray Burnett. Est. 1975. Short stories, poetry, criticism. Policy is explicitly socialist and articles are mostly concerned with political issues. Literary contents deal with writing in a cultural minority and aim to introduce Gaelic writers to a broader non-Gaelic audience.

Chapman
118 Brankholm Brae, Hamilton, Lanarkshire.
Three times a year. Poetry, short stories, critical and philosophical articles. Prose contributions up to 6000 words.

Gairm
29 Waterloo Street, Glasgow G2 6B2.
Editor, Derick S. Thomson. Est. 1951. Quarterly. Gaelic poetry, fiction, current affairs, criticism and reviews.

Lallans
174 Craigleith Road, Edinburgh EH4 2EE.
Editor, J. K. Annand. Est. 1973. Twice a year. Writing in Lowland Scots. Short stories, poetry, articles, literary criticism. Prose contributions up to 2500 words.

Leopard Magazine
154 Union Street, Aberdeen.
Editor, Diane Morgan. Est. 1974. Monthly. A lively regional magazine with high literary standards. Articles deal with life past and present in Aberdeen and the North-East.

Library Review
30 Clydeholm Road, Glasgow G14 0BJ.
Editor, W. R. Aitken. Quarterly. A journal for the library profession but its literary articles and extensive book reviews have a wide general interest.

Lines Review
Edgefield Road, Loanhead, Midlothian.

Editor, Robert Calder. Est. 1952. Quarterly. Devoted to new poetry, with occasional critical articles and book reviews, *Lines* has a distinguished record of discovering new writers and printing verse by all the leading Scottish poets.

New Edinburgh Review
1 Buccleuch Place, Edinburgh 8.

Published by the Edinburgh University Publications Board from the same street in which the original *Edinburgh Review* was founded. The *NER* sometimes succeeds in being as electrifying as its predecessor. Its attitudes and approach tend to change under different editors but its critical articles and creative contributions are always stimulating.

Prospice
9 Scullamus, Breakish, Isle of Skye IV42 8QB.

Editors, J. C. R. Green and Michael Edwards. Est. 1973. Three times a year. Most issues are devoted to specific themes (French poetry, Italian poetry, etc.) and to commissioned articles. Some unsolicited poetry is accepted.

Q (Question)
58 Queen Street, Edinburgh EH2 3NS.

Editor, Peter Cheine. Est. 1975. Fortnightly. An independent political review also covering the arts, business and science. Book reviews. Contributions up to 1500 words.

Scotia Review
3 Moray Street, Wick, Caithness.

Editor, David Morrison. Three times a year. A literary review "for the Scottish Muse and Nation." Poetry, fiction, comment, book reviews.

The Scots Magazine
D. C. Thomson & Co., Ltd., Bank Street, Dundee DD1 9HU.

Editor, Maurice Fleming. Est. 1739. Monthly. Scotland's oldest magazine, with a worldwide circulation. Articles of general Scottish interest, some poetry and occasional fiction. Colour and black-and-white photographs.

Scottish Educational Journal
46 Moray Place, Edinburgh EH3 6BH.

Editor, Angus McIntyre. Est. 1876. Weekly. Education, Scottish writing, poetry, short stories by established writers of interest to teachers.

Scottish Field
Allander House, 137 Leith Walk, Edinburgh EH6 8NS.

Editor, Roderick Martine. Est. 1903. Monthly. Leisure pursuits, topography, the arts, history, sport. Illustrated in colour and black-and-white. Contributions up to 1500 words.

Scottish Literary Journal
Department of English, University of Aberdeen, Old Aberdeen AB9 2UB.

Editor, Thomas Crawford. Twice a year. A review of studies in Scottish language and literature.

The Scottish Review
24 George Square, Glasgow G2 1EF.

Managing Editor, Lindsay Whyte. Est. 1975. Quarterly. Published by the Scottish Civic Trust and the Saltire Society. A wide-ranging review of the arts and the environment. Poetry, short stories, book reviews.

Newspapers

The main Scottish daily newspapers have a generally high standard of feature articles dealing with topical and Scottish subjects. Each paper has its own character and style and those with weekend magazine sections cover a wide range of interests.

Dundee Courier and Advertiser
7 Bank Street, Dundee DD1 9HV.

Evening Express
Long Stracht, Mastrick, Aberdeen AB9 1YT.

Evening News
North Bridge, Edinburgh EH1 1YT.

Evening Telegraph and Post
Courier Place, Dundee DD1 9QJ.

Evening Times
70 Mitchell Street, Glasgow G1 3LZ.

Glasgow Herald
70 Mitchell Street, Glasgow G1 3LZ.

Greenock Telegraph
2 Crawford Street, Greenock.

Paisley Daily Express
20 New Street, Paisley.

Press and Journal
Long Stracht, Mastrick, Aberdeen AB9 8AF.

The Scotsman
North Bridge, Edinburgh EH1 1YT.

Pen Names

Anderson, Ella	MacLeod, Ellen Jane
Bannatyne, Jack	Gaston, William James
Black, Gavin	Wynd, Oswald
Calder, Ritchie	Ritchie-Calder, Lord
Calvin, Henry	Hanley, Clifford
Christie, Guy	Christie, Arthur Galafries
Crawford, Robert	Rae, Hugh C.
Dallas, John	Duncan, William Murdoch
Devine, Dominic	Devine, David McDonald
Drinan, Adam	MacLeod, Joseph
Flower, Jake	Bold, Alan
Fraser, Jane	Pilcher, Rosamonde
Graham, Neill	Duncan, William Murdoch
Halliday, Dorothey	Dunnett, Dorothy
Kay, Ada F.	Stewart, A. J.
Lochinvar	Fenwick, Hubert
MacCall, Isobel	Orr, Elizabeth Boyd
MacLeod, Robert	Knox, William
Sandison, Janet	Duncan, Jane
Stuart, Ian	Maclean, Alistair
Webster, Noah	Knox, William
Yuill, P. B.	Williams, Gordon and Terry Venables

Living Scottish Writers

THE information contained in this section is confined to living Scottish writers and to writers who have for long resided in Scotland.

In most cases the particulars have been provided by the authors themselves but when this has not been possible, through failure to make contact, the information has been compiled from other sources without, it is hoped, serious inaccuracies. For personal reasons some writers have preferred not to be included but any inadvertent omissions will be rectified in future editions if brought to the attention of the editor.

Adam, James S.
Born Dundee. Started in newspapers on the *Scottish Daily Express* advertisement department. After serving as a staff officer during the War became successively features editor of the Glasgow *Evening News*, *Daily Record*, asst. editor *Evening Times*, editor *Weekly Scotsman* and *Scottish TV Guide*. Moved into management as general manager of The Scotsman Publications Ltd.; subsequently managing director of the *Chester Chronicle* and then *Middlesburgh Evening Gazette*. Past Pres., Scottish Federation of Sea Anglers, Scottish Canoe Assoc. Member Scottish Council of Physical Recreation and Cairngorms Winter Sports Development Board. Organiser of the International Gathering of the Clans, 1977.

Con. to Alastair Maclean's Scotland (1973, Deutsch). A Fell Fine Baker (1975, Hutchinson). The Spirit of Scotland (1977, Ramsay Head Press).

4 Southlawn Court, Easter Park, Barnton, Edinburgh EH4 6JR.

Aitken, Adam Jack
Born Edinburgh 1921. Educ. Lasswade Secondary School; Edinburgh Univ. Assisted Sir William Craigie on A Dictionary of the Older Scottish Tongue from 1948 and became editor in 1956. Senior Lecturer, 1971, Reader in English Language, 1975, Edinburgh Univ. Member exec. council Scottish National Dictionary Assoc. Member of council, Scottish Text Soc. Chairman, Language Com. Assoc. of Scottish Literary Studies.

Edit. A Dictionary of the Older Scottish Tongue, Vol. 3 (1964, Univ. Chicago Press); Vol. 4 (1972); Parts 27-28 (1975). Co-edit., Edinburgh Studies in English and Scots (1971, Longman). Co-edit., The Computer and Literary Studies (1973, Edinburgh Univ. Press). Edit., Lowland Scots (1973, Assoc. for Scottish Literary Studies).

13 Lockharton Gardens, Edinburgh EH14 2AU. 031-443 7755.

Aitken, William Russell
Born Calderbank, Lanarkshire, 1913. Educ. Dunfermline High School, Edinburgh Univ. RAF 1941-46. Successively County Librarian Clackmannanshire, Perth and Kinross and Ayrshire. Joined staff of Scottish School of Librarianship, 1962. Reader, Dept. of Librarianship, Strathclyde Univ. Editor *Library Review* 1964- . Pres. Scottish Library Assoc., 1965. Hon. Pres. University of Stirling Bibliographical Soc., 1974.

Edit. Poems in Scots and English by William Soutar (1961, Oliver & Boyd; 1975, Scot. Academic Press). A History of the Public Library Movement in Scotland (1971, Scot. Library Assoc.). Checklists of the writings of Hugh MacDiarmid, Neil Gunn Fionn Mac Colla, Sydney Goodsir Smith.

6 Tannahill Terrace, Dunblane, Perthshire FK15 0AX.

Alexander, Kenneth John Wilson
Born Edinburgh 1927. Educ. George Heriot's, Edinburgh; School of Economics, Dundee. Has held posts at Universities of Leeds, Sheffield, Aberdeen. Since 1963 Professor of Economics, Univ. of Strathclyde. Chairman, Highlands and Islands Development Board; President, Saltire Society.

The Economist in Business (1967, Blackwell). Fairfields: A Study in Industrial Change (1970, Allen Lane). The Political Economy of Change (1975, Blackwell).

Ardnacraggan, Callander, Perthshire. Callander 303077.

Allan, John R.
Born Aberdeenshire. Educ. Aberdeen Univ. For some years journalist in Glasgow.

Farmer's Boy (1935, Methuen). Summer in Scotland (1938, Methuen). North East Lowlands of Scotland (2nd edit., 1974, Hale).

Anderson, Alasdair
Born Yorkshire 1943. Brought up in Scotland and educated "after a fashion." Trained as an illustrator/designer. Worked for some years in London as a freelance artist on children's books, Television, newspapers and magazines. Now a school teacher in Midlothian.

The Queen of Hearts (1973, Dobson). The Chewy Toffee Man Story (1976, Dobson).

1 Outerston Cottages, Temple, by Gorebridge, Midlothian. Temple 212.

Angus, David
Born Brora 1925. Educ. Inverness Academy, Lanark Grammar School, Edinburgh Univ., Moray House. Served in Royal Navy 1943-46. Taught English in Beath High School (1951-59) and Alloa Academy (1961-71). Hon. Sec. Forth Branch, Saltire Society.

Roses and Thorns: Scottish Teenage Verse (1972, Club Leabhar). The Edinburgh Wax Museum (1976). Edit. Windings, a poetry anthology for schools, and Hop Scotch, an anthology in prose and verse (1976, Holmes McDougall). Verse in various magazines.

122 Henderson Street, Bridge of Allan, Stirling. Bridge of Allan 2306.

Annand, J. K.
Born Edinburgh 1908. Educ. Broughton Sec., Edinburgh Univ. Served in Royal Navy 1941-46. Married, four daughters. Retired teacher. Editor of *Lallans*.

Sing it Aince for Pleisure (1965, Macdonald). Two Voices (1968, Macdonald). Edit. Early Lyrics by Hugh MacDiarmid (1968, Akros). Twice for Joy (1973, Macdonald). Poems and Translations (1975, Akros).

174 Craigleith Road, Edinburgh. 031-332 6905.

Barrow, G. W. S.
Born Leeds 1924. Educ. St Edward's School, Oxford; Inverness Royal Academy; St Andrews Univ.; Pembroke Coll., Oxford. Professor of Scottish History, St Andrews.

Feudal Britain (1956). Acts of Malcolm IV, King of Scots (1960). Robert Bruce and the Community of the Realm of Scotland (1965, revised edit. 1976). Acts of William I.

Bennett, Douglas M.
Born Edinburgh, 1944. Educ. Edinburgh Univ. Engineer and part-time artist.

Many booklets published by Romar Press including Sylivia I and II (1972, 1973) and Sermons of the Sorcer (1974).

Romar Cottage, Fountainhall, Stow, Midlothian. Fountainhall 252.

Bermant, Chaim
Born Lithuania. Came to Scotland when he was eight. Many of his novels reflect the Jewish way of life in Glasgow.

74

Jericho Sleep Alone (1964, Chapman & Hall). Ben Preserve Us (1965). Diary of an Old Man (1966). The Second Mrs Whitberg (1976, Allen & Unwin). Coming Home (1976, Allen & Unwin).

Bingham, Caroline
Born London 1938. Educ. Cheltenham Ladies' College, Bristol Univ. Council member, Royal Stewart Soc.

The Making of a King: The Early Years of James VI and I (1968, Collins). James V, King of Scots (1969, Collins). The Life and Times of Edward II (1973, Weidenfeld). The Stewart Kingdom of Scotland, 1371-1603 (1974, Weidenfeld). The Kings and Queens of Scotland (1976, Weidenfeld).

King James VI of Scotland I of England, a recital programme, was performed at the Edinburgh Festival, 1975.

199 Prince of Wales Road, London NW5 3QB. 01-267 0240.

Black, David
Born Wynberg, South Africa, 1941.

Theory of Diet (1966, Turret Books). With Decorum (1967, Scorpion Press). A Dozen Short Poems (1968, Turret Books). The Educators (1969, Barrie & Jenkins). The Old Hag (1972, Akros). The Happy Crow (1974, Lines Review Editions).

Boase, Alan M.
Born St Andrews 1902. Educ. Eton; New College, Oxford; Trinity, Cambridge. Asst. Lecturer, Sheffield Univ., 1929-36. Professor of Modern Languages, Univ. College, Southampton, 1937-65. Marshall Professor of French, Glasgow Univ. 1969.

The Fortunes of Montaigne: A History of the Essays in France, 1580-1669 (1935, Methuen). Edit. Jean de Sponde: Poesies (1949, Pierre Coiller, Geneva). Edit. Jean de Sponde Meditations (1954, Corte, Paris). Poetry of France, Vol I, 1400-1600 (1964, Methuen). Vol II 1600-1800 (1975, Methuen). Vol III 1800-1900 (1976, Methuen). Vol IV 1900-1965 (1969, Methuen).

39 Inverleith Place, Edinburgh EH3 5QD. 031-352 3005.

Bold, Alan
Born Edinburgh 1943. Educ. Broughton School, Edinburgh Univ. Worked on *Times Educational Supplement* (*Scotland*) and since 1967 has been full-time writer and artist. Married to an art teacher; one daughter. Organised two exhibitions: Scottish Realism (1971) and Bellamy-Dallas-Brown-Gillon-Moffat (1975). Has also held one-man exhibitions of Illuminated Poems.

Society Inebrious (1965, Mowat Hamilton). The Voyage (1966, Macdonald). To Find the New (1967, Chatto). A Perpetual Motion Machine (1969, Chatto). The State of the Nation (1969, Chatto). He Will be Greatly Missed (1971, Turret). A Century of People (1971, Academy Editions). The Auld Stymie (1971, Akros). A Pint of Bitter (1971, Chatto). A Lunar Event (1973, Keepsake). Hammer and Thistle (1974, Caithness Books). Thom Gunn and Ted Hughes (Oliver & Boyd, 1976).

East Lodge, Balbirnie Estate, Markinch, Fife. Glenrothes 758031.

Bolton, Frederic James (Deric Bolton)
Born Paisley, 1908. Educ. Shrewsbury and Birkbeck College, London Univ. Research chemist. Technical director J. F. Macfarlane & Co., Ltd., Edinburgh, 1937-62. Convener, Edin. Frontier Group. Vice-chairman, Scot. Assoc. for Speaking of Verse, 1970-73. Chairman, Soc. of Chemical Industry, Edin. Section, 1951-53, 1972-74.

A view from Benmore (1972, Outposts). Glasgow Central Station (1972, Outposts). The Wild Uncharted Country: A Scientific Pilgrimage (1973, Outposts).

17 Wester Coates Avenue, Edinburgh EH12 5LS. 031-337 2182.

Bowie, Janetta H.
Born Greenock 1907. Educ. Greenock High School, Glasgow Univ., Jordanhill Coll.

Has been Infants Teacher, Principal Teacher in Remedial Subjects and also evening teacher in Greenock Prison Borstal Section. Founder Greenock Writers' Club and Scot. Assoc. of Writers (now Vice-pres.). Former Vice-pres., Greenock Camera Club.

Penny Buff (1975, Constable). Penny Boss (1976, Constable). Third book of the trilogy in preparation. Radio plays for children, stories, talks, discussions.

32 Fox Street, Greenock.

Boyd, Edward
Born Stevenston, Ayrshire, 1916. Educ. Stevenston Higher Grade School and Ardrossan Academy. Served in Royal Air Force 1939-45.

The Dark Number, with Roger Parkes (1973, Constable). This was also published in German as Der dunkle Engel by Wilhelm Goldmann Verlag Munchen. In French as Le Fil Rompu by Editions Opta, Paris where it was awarded the Grand Prix de la Litterature Policiere for 1975. In America it was published by Walker & Company, New York. An Italian edition is due to be published shortly. The View From Daniel Pike, with Bill Knox (1974, Hutchinson). Also published in America.

Radio: Enough Fingers To Make A Hand. The Wolf Far Hence (Screen Writers' Guild Award). The Candle of Darkness. The House of Winter. The Forest of Error. The Runnable Stag. Badger by Owl-Light.

Television: The Odd Man (series) (Screen Writers' Guild Award). A Black Candle for Mrs Gogarty. The Lower Largo Sequence. The Fell Sergeant. The View From Daniel Pike. Good Morning, Yesterday.

Films: Robbery (1967) co-winner of Screen Writers' Guild Award. Hennessy (1975).

32 Minerva Street, Glasgow G3. 041-221 7892.

Boyd, Elizabeth Orr (Mrs Norman Story)
Born Largs 1912. Educ. Largs High School, Ardrossan Academy, Glasgow Univ. One of the founders of the Saltire Society and Treasurer for first five years.

Cross-Country Walks in North-West Highlands (1952, Oliver & Boyd).

Radio talks and articles in Scottish press.

17 Burnt Firs Place, Heathhall, Dumfries.

Brown, George Mackay
Born Stromness 1921. Educ. Stromness Academy, Newbattle Abbey, Edinburgh Univ.

The Storm (1954, Orkney Press). Loaves and Fishes: Poems (1959, Hogarth Press). The Year of the Whale: Poems (1965, Hogarth Press). A Calendar of Love: Stories (1967, Hogarth Press). A Time to Keep: Stories (1969, Hogarth Press). An Orkney Tapestry: Essays (1969, Gollancz). A Spell for Green Corn: Play (1970, Hogarth Press). Fishermen with Ploughs: Poems (1971, Hogarth Press). Poems New and Selected (1971, Hogarth Press). Greenvoe: Novel (1972, Hogarth Press). Magnus: Novel (1973, Hogarth Press). Hawkfall: Stories (1974, Hogarth Press). The Two Fiddlers: Stories (1974, Hogarth Press). Letters from Hamnavoe: Essays (1975, Gordon Wright). Winterfold: Poems (1976, Hogarth Press). The Sun's Net: Stories (1976, Hogarth Press). Pictures in the Cave: Stories (1976, Hogarth Press).

Plays: A Spell for Green Corn, Radio 3, 1967, first stage production by Strathclyde University Players.

Orkney, A Trilogy of Stories, has been produced on television and a great volume of work has been broadcast on radio.

3 Mayburn Court, Stromness, Orkney.

Brown, Raymond Lamont
Born Yorkshire, of Scottish parents, 1939. MA, AMIET, FRGS, MRAS, MJS, FSA (Scot). Spent six years in industry. Travelled widely in the Far East as historian/researcher. Became freelance author in 1965. Founder Japan Research Projects.

History of St Mark's Church, Dewsbury (1965, Birkdale). Clarinda (1966, Black). A Book of Epitaphs (1967, David & Charles). Sir Walter Scott's Letters on Witchcraft and Demonology (1969, SRP). Robert Burns's Commonplace Book (1970, SRP). A Book of Superstitions (1972, David & Charles). A Book of Proverbs (1972, David & Charles). A Book of Witchcraft (1972, David & Charles). Charles Kirkpatrick Sharpe's History of Witchcraft in Scotland (1973, SRP). The General Trades of Berwick on Tweed, 1894 (1973, Bell). Robert Burns's Tour of the Borders (1973, Boydell). Robert Burns's Tour of the Highlands (1973, Boydell). Phantoms, Legends, Customs and Superstitions of the Sea (1973, Patrick Stephens). A New Book of Epitaphs (1973, Graham). Casebook of Military Mystery (1974, PSL). The Magic Oracles of Japan (1974, Fowler).

Various scripts on folklore for radio and television.

25 Ladywell Road, Tweedmouth, Berwick-upon-Tweed. Berwick 7650.

Bruce, David
Born Dundee 1939. Educ. Dundee High School, Aberdeen Grammar, Edinburgh Univ. Deputy Director, Scottish Council for Educational Technology/Scottish Film Council. Former director Edinburgh Film Festival. Married, two children.

Sun Pictures: The Hill-Adamson Calotypes (1973, Studio Vista).

6 Maclachlan Place, Helensburgh G84 9BZ. 0436 5220.

Bruce, George
Born Fraserburgh, 1909. Educ. Fraserburgh Academy, Aberdeen Univ. 1933-34, Aberdeen College of Educ. 1935-46, Asst. Master then Deputy Headmaster, English Dept., Dundee High School. 1947-56, Programme Producer, BBC Aberdeen. 1956-70, Talks Producer (Documentary), BBC Edinburgh with special responsibility in radio and TV for Arts Programme. 1971-73, First Fellow in Creative Writing at Glasgow Univ.

Sea Talk: Poems (1944, Maclellan). Selected Poems (1947, Saltire Soc.). Landscapes and Figures: Poems (1967, Akros). Collected Poems (1970, Edin. Univ. Press. Scottish Arts Council Award). The City of Edinburgh (1973, Pitkin). Anne Redpath (1974, Edin. Univ. Press). Festival in the North (1975, Hale). Some Practical Good (1976, Cockburn Assoc.). Edit., with Maurice Lindsay and Edwin Morgan, annual Scottish Poetry anthology. Represented in numerous anthologies of verse.

1974, Visiting Professor at Theological Seminary, Richmond, Virginia; Writer in Residence at Prescott College, Arizona. 1975, Lecture tour in USA. 1976-77, Visiting Professor of English at Wooster College, Ohio. On editorial board *Scottish Review*.

Regular series on BBC Radio included Scottish Life and Letters, Arts Review and annual Burns' and St Andrew's Day programmes. With Maurice Lindsay edited Scotland's first television magazine of the arts, Counterpoint.

Bryden, Bill
Born Greenock 1942. Educ. Greenock High School. Assistant Director, Royal Court Theatre, London, 1968. Assistant Director, Royal Lyceum Theatre, Edinburgh, 1970-74. Associate Director, National Theatre, 1974- . Governor Royal Scottish Academy of Music and Drama.

Willie Rough (1971, Southside). Benny Lynch (1973, Southside).

Plays: Willie Rough (1972, Lyceum, Edin.). Benny Lynch (1974, Lyceum).
Benny Lynch was produced on Granada TV, and Willie Rough on BBC TV in 1976. A Whip Round for the Driver was broadcast on BBC Radio in 1972.

13 Allfarthing Lane, London SW18. 01-874 4592.

Buchan, Tom
Born Glasgow, 1931. Educ. Glasgow Univ. Lecturer, theatre director, festival director, editor.

Ikons (1957, Tambaram Press). Dolphins at Cochin (1969, Barrie & Jenkins). Exorcism (1972, Midnight Press; 1975, Facet Press). Poems, 1969-72 (1972, Poni Press).

Plays: Tell Charlie Thanks for the Truss (1972, Traverse Theatre, Edinburgh). Knox and Mary (1972, Pool Theatre, Edinburgh). The Great Northern Welly Boot Show (1972, King's Theatre, Glasgow).

10 Pittville Street, Edinburgh EH15 2BY. 031-669 8235.

Butter, Peter Herbert
Born Coldstream 1921. Educ. Charterhouse; Balliol College, Oxford. Regius Professor of English, Glasgow Univ. since 1965.

Shelley's Idols of the Cave (1954, Edin. Univ. Press). Francis Thompson (1961, Longman). Edwin Muir (1962, Oliver & Boyd). Edwin Muir, Man and Poet (1966, Oliver & Boyd). Edit. Shelley's Alastor, Prometheus Unbound and other Poems (1971, Collins). Edit. Selected Letters of Edwin Muir (1974, Hogarth Press).

Ashfield, Bridge of Weir, Renfrewshire PA11 3AW. Bridge of Weir 613139.

Caird, James Bowman
Born West Linton, 1913. Educ. Boroughmuir School, Edinburgh Univ., Sorbonne. Taught in Wick, Edinburgh, Peebles. Army service, 1940-46. HMI (Dumfries, Glasgow, Stirling, Ross and Cromarty) 1947-74. Vice-president, Assoc. for Scottish Literary Studies.

Lewis Grassic Gibbon in Essays in Literature (1935, Oliver & Boyd). Fergusson and Stevenson in Robert Fergusson, 1950-74 (1952, Nelson). Neil Gunn, Novelist of the North (1964, Caithness County Council). Neil Gunn and Scottish Fiction in Neil M. Gunn, the Man and the Writer (1973, Blackwood). Fionn Maccolla, The Twofold Heritage (1973, Caithness Books).

1 Drummond Crescent, Inverness. Inverness 32858.

Caird, Janet (nee Kirkwood)
Born Livingstonia, Malawi, 1913. Educ. Dollar Academy, Edinburgh Univ., Grenoble Univ., Sorbonne. Married James B. Caird 1938, two daughters. Professional teacher.

Angus the Tartan Partan: Children's (1961, Bles). Murder Reflected (1965, Bles). Perturbing Spirit (1966, Bles). Murder Scholastic (1966, Bles). The Loch (1967, Bles). Murder Remote (1968, Bles). Also writes poetry and short stories.

1 Drummond Crescent, Inverness. Inverness 32858.

Callison, Brian
Born Manchester 1934. Educ. Dundee High School, Dundee College of Art. Early years in Merchant Navy. Studied design at College of Art then entered commercial field. Has been managing director of construction company and general manager of large entertainment centre. Head of Dundee Unit of Royal Naval Auxiliary Service. Sails his own 70 foot yacht (Ketch).

A Flock of Ships (1970, Collins). A Plague of Sailors (1971, Collins). The Dawn Attack (1972, Collins). A Web of Salvage (1973, Collins). Trapp's War (1974, Collins). A Ship is Dying (1976, Collins).

1 Margaret Crescent, Est Ferry, Dundee. Dundee 77392.

Campbell, Donald
Born Wick 1940. After "uncomfortable education" in Edinburgh, served apprenticeship as bank clerk, then left Scotland for four years working at various jobs, mostly in London. Returned to Edinburgh in 1964 and for ten years worked as accounts clerk. Began to publish 1969. Writer in Residence, Edinburgh Schools, 1974- . Member of The Heretics, Lallans Society and Edinburgh Theatre Workshop.

Poems: (1971, Akros). Rhymes 'n Reasons (1972, Reprographia). Murals (1975, Lothlorien). Sonnets frae Siberia (1976, Lothlorien). Writes regular column in *Scots Independent*.

Plays: The Jesuit (1976, Traverse Theatre, Edinburgh). Fletcher (1975, won special prize from Arts in Fife).

53 Viewforth, Edinburgh. 031-229 1862.

Campbell, Ian
Born Lausanne 1942. Educ. schools in Switzerland and Scotland, Aberdeen Univ., Edinburgh Univ. Son of minister of Scots Kirk, Lausanne. Since 1967 lecturer in English literature at Edinburgh Univ. Teaching experience in Canada, USA, Germany, and research activities in North America and Switzerland. Vice-president Carlyle Society. Council member ASLS. Member UCSL.

Co-editor, with R. D. S. Jack, Jamie the Saxt (1970, Calder). Co-editor of the Duke-Edinburgh edition of The Correspondence of Thomas and Jane Carlyle (1970, Vols 1-4; 1976, Vols 5-7; ongoing, about 40 vols in all. Duke Univ. Press, Durham, NC). Edit. New Everyman edition of Carlyle's Reminiscences (1972, Dent). New introduction to Everyman edition Carlyle's Selected Essays (1972, Dent). Thomas Carlyle (1974, Hamilton). Edit. Critical Essays on Nineteenth Century Scottish Fiction (1977, Carcanet Press).

Reviews for various journals. Scripts for BBC Scotland, BBC World Radio, Border TV.

Dept. of English Literature, University of Edinburgh, Hume Tower, George Square, Edinburgh EH8 9JX. 031-667 1011.

Campbell of Canna, John Lorne
Born 1906. Owns and farms Isle of Canna, Inner Hebrides. Married 1935, Margaret Fay, author of Folksongs and Folklore of South Uist. Educ. Cargilfield, Rugby; St John's College, Oxford—D.Litt 1965. Hon. LLD, St Francis Xavier Univ., Antigonish, NS. Hon. D.Litt., Glasgow Univ.

Highland Songs of the Forty-Five (1933). The Book of Barra, with Compton Mackenzie and Carl Borgstrom (1936). Sia Sgialachdan (1938). Act Now for the Highlands, with Sir Alexander MacEwen (1939). Gaelic in Scottish Education and Life (1945). Gaelic Folksongs from the Isle of Barra, with Annie Johnston and John MacLean (1950). Father Allan McDonald of Eriskay (1954). Stories from South Uist (1961). The Furrow Behind Me: The Autobiography of a Hebridean Crofter (1962). Edward Lhuyd in the Scottish Highlands, with Derick Thomson (1963). A School in South Uist (1964). Strange Things, with Trevor H. Hall (1968). Hebridean Folk Songs, with F. Collinson (1969—Vols 2 and 3 in preparation). Macrolepidoptera Cannae (1970). Saoghal an Treobhiche (1972). Edit. A Collection of Highland Rites and Customs (1975).

Chisnall, Edward H.
Born Bellshill 1942. Post-graduate student Glasgow School of Art. Freelanced in London. Principal teacher in Motherwell. Resigned to take family to France and live off painting. Now working from Elgin.

Has written a series of plays for Glasgow Close Theatre and radio broadcasts. Poems in literary magazines.

Christie, Arthur Galafres (Guy Christie)
Born Rothesay 1901. Educ. Rothesay Academy, West of Scotland Agricultural Coll. Took up journalism in 1924. After serving on various journals became Scottish Office PRO at St Andrews House. Retired 1962. Wrote widely on yachting and broadcast regularly on BBC. Edited Scottish Yachtsman.

Harbours of the Forth (1955 Chris. Johnson). Storeys of Lancaster (1964, Collins). Crieff Hydro 1868-1968 (1967, Oliver & Boyd).

61 Comiston Road, Edinburgh EH10 6AG. 031-447 2736.

Clark of Heriotshall, Arthur Melville
Born Edinburgh 1895. Educ. Stewart's Coll.; Edinburgh Univ.; Oriel Coll., Oxford. Lecturer in English, Reading Univ. Reader in English, Edinburgh Univ. External examiner in English, Aberdeen and St Andrews Univ. Editor, Edinburgh Univ. Calendar. Farmer and member of Scottish Landowners' Fed. Exhibitor at RSA. D.Litt., D.Phil., FRSE, FRSA, Knight of St Lazarus of Jerusalem, Knight of Polonia Restituta.

The Realistic Revolt in Modern Poetry (1922, Blackwell). Thomas Heywood, Playwright and Miscellanist (1931, Blackwell; 1967, Russell & Russell). Autobiography, its

Genesis and Phases (1935, Oliver & Boyd). Spoken English (1946, Oliver & Boyd). Studies in Literary Modes (1946, Oliver & Boyd). Sonnets from the French and other Poems (1966, Oliver & Boyd). Sir Walter Scott, the Formative Years (1969, Blackwood). 3 Woodburn Terrace, Edinburgh EH10 4SH. 031-447 1240.

Clark, Thomas A.
Born 1944.
Poetry: Down and Out in Tighnabruaich (1970, Akros). Some Particulars (1971). Pointing Still (1974). The Garden (1974). Four Flowers (1974).

Conn, Stewart
Born Glasgow 1936. Radio Drama Dept., BBC Scotland. Scottish Arts Council Drama Panel 1970-73. Literary Adviser, Royal Lyceum Theatre, Edinburgh, 1973-75.
Poetry: Interrogation (1958, privately). Thunder in the Air (1967, Akros). The Chinese Tower (1967, Macdonald). Stoats in the Sunlight (1968, Hutchinson—Scottish Arts Council Poetry Award). An Ear to the Ground (1972, Hutchinson—Poetry Book Society Choice).
Plays: The King, in New English Dramatists 14 (1970, Penguin). Fancy Seeing You, Then, in Educational Playbill (1969, Hutchinson). The Burning (1973, Calder & Boyars). The Aquarium and Other Plays (1976, Calder & Boyars).
Recent stage plays include Thistlewood (1975, Traverse Theatre, Edinburgh) and Count Your Blessings (1975, Pitlochry Festival Theatre). Other productions include Break-Down (1961, Citizens Theatre, Glasgow). Broche (1968, Edinburgh Univ. Drama Soc.). A Slight Touch of the Sun (1972, Pool Theatre, Edinburgh). Many radio and television plays and adaptations.
Radio Drama Dept., BBC Broadcasting House, Queen Street, Edinburgh.

Cook, Robert Leslie
Born Edinburgh 1921. Educ. Gilsland Park School, George Watson's Coll., Edinburgh Univ. Royal Navy 1939-52. Married, two daughters.
Hebrides Overture and other Poems (1948, Plewlands Press). Within the Tavern Caught (1952, Hand and Flower Press). Sometimes a Word (1963, Plewlands Press). Time with a Drooping Hand (1976, Outposts).
Edit. Fleet Poetry Broadsheet (1944-46). Co-edit. New Athenian Broadsheet (1947-48) and Windfall (1955).
45 Plewlands Gardens, Edinburgh EH10 5JT.

Cooper, Dominic Xavier
Born Winchester 1944. Educ. Ampleforth Coll.; Magdalen Coll., Oxford. 1966-70 worked with record company and publishing house in London. 1970-72, taught in language school in Reykjavik, Iceland. 1972-73, worked as labourer on roads in Isle of Mull and wrote. 1973- worked as clockmaker in Edinburgh.
The Dead of Winter (1975, Chatto). Sunrise (1977, Chatto).
7 Well Court, Dean Village, Edinburgh EH4 3BE. 031-225 4878.

Copeland, James
Ex-salmon poacher, policeman, river bailiff, actor and poet.
A Few Poems (Bruce and Watson). Some Work (Bramma Publications).

Cowan, Evelyn, Mrs
Born in the Gorbals, Glasgow, 1926, of Lithuanian parents. Educ. Strathbungo Secondary School and adult evening classes. Youngest of family of eleven children. On committee of Glasgow Writers Club. Former chairman Scottish branch of Pioneer Women of Israel.
Spring Remembered (1974, Canongate). Portrait of Alice (1976, Canongate).
As a working journalist has written a regular features column for many years. Over a dozen short stories broadcast.
12 Rostan Road, Glasgow G43 2XF. 041-637 4013.

Craig, David
Born Aberdeen 1932. Educ. Aberdeen Grammar School, Aberdeen Univ., Cambridge Univ. Married, one daughter, three sons. Taught in Scottish schools 1958-59; Univ. of Ceylon, 1959-61; Workers Educ. Assoc., 1961-64. Lancaster Univ., 1964- . Editor, *Fireweed*, quarterly.

Scottish Literature and the Scottish People, 1680-1830 (1961, Chatto). Edit. Moderne Prosa und Lyrik der Britischen Inseln (1968, Aufbau Verlag, Berlin). Edit. Dickens's Hard Times (1969, Penguin). Edit. Hugh MacDiarmid's Selected Poems (1970, Penguin). The Real Foundations: Literature and Social Change (1973, Chatto). Edit. Marxists on Literature (1975, Pelican). Poems and stories in various journals.
Play: Common Will Against the Giant (1975, Unity Theatre, London).
107 Bowerham Road, Lancaster. Lancaster 66893.

Cronin, Archibald Joseph
Born 1896. Educ. Glasgow Univ. MD. Worked in Glasgow hospitals. Practised in South Wales, 1921-24, London, 1926-30, after which he devoted himself to writing. Now lives in Switzerland.

Hatter's Castle (1931). Three Loves (1932). Grand Canary (1933). Stars Look Down (1935). Citadel (1937). Keys of the Kingdom (1942). Green Years (1944). Shannon's Way (1948). Spanish Gardener (1950). Adventures in Two Worlds (1952). Beyond this Place (1953). Crusader's Tomb (1956). The Northern Light (1958). The Judas Tree (1961). Song for Sixpence (1964). Pocketful of Rye (1969). Gollancz.
Creator of the television series Dr Finlay's Case Book.

Czerkawska, Catherine Lucy
Born Leeds 1950. Educ. Leeds, Ayr, Kilwinning, Edinburgh Univ., Leeds Univ. Worked for a time in New 57 Art Gallery, Edinburgh. At present about nine months in the year in Finland teaching English to businessmen.

Seven New Voices: Poems (1972, Garret Arts). White Boats: Poems, with Andrew Greig (1973, Garret Arts). Fisherfolk of Carrick (1975, Molendinar Press). A Book of Men: Poems (1976, Akros).
Radio Plays: The Hare and the Fox. A Bit of a Wilderness.
6 Elms Way, Laurel Bank, Maybole, Ayrshire. Maybole 82014.

Daiches, David
Born Edinburgh 1912. Educ. George Watson's Coll., Edinburgh; Edinburgh Univ.; Balliol Coll., Oxford. Asst. Prof. of English, Univ. of Chicago, 1939-43. Prof. of English, Cornell Univ., 1946-51. Fellow of Jesus Coll., Cambridge, 1951-61. Now Prof. of English, Univ. of Sussex.

The Place and Meaning of Poetry (1935). Literary Values (1936). Literature and Society (1938). Poetry and the Modern World (1940). Robert Louis Stevenson (1947). Robert Burns (1950). Willa Cather (1941). Critical Approaches to Literature (1956). Two Worlds (1956). John Milton (1957). Critical History of English Literature (1960). The Paradox of Scottish Culture (1964). Some Late Victorian Attitudes (1969). Scotch Whisky (1969). Sir Walter Scott and His World (1971). A Third World (1971). Penguin Companion to Literature: Britain and the Commonwealth (1971). Robert Burns and His World (1971). Charles Edward Stewart (1973). R. L. Stevenson and His World (1973). Was (1975). Moses (1975).
Downsview, Wellhouse Lane, Burgess Hill, Sussex.

Darling, Sir Frank Fraser
Born 1903. Educ. Midland Agricultural Coll.; Edinburgh Univ.

Island Years (1940). The Story of Scotland (1942). Island Farm (1943). Natural History of the Highlands and Islands (1947). Many works on ecology and natural history.

Davie, Elspeth
Born Kilmarnock. Educ. Edinburgh Univ., Edinburgh Coll. of Art, Moray House. Taught painting in the Borders, Aberdeen and Edinburgh. After marriage lived for several years in Ireland before returning to Scotland.

Providings: novel (1965, Calder & Boyars). The Spark: short stories (1968, Calder & Boyars). Creating a Scene: novel (1971, Calder & Boyars). Short stories in several anthologies.

15 Leven Terrace, Edinburgh.

Davis, Margaret Thomson
Born Bathgate. Educ. Albert Sec. School, Glasgow. Scottish Com. PEN.

The Breadmakers (1972, Allison & Busby). A Baby Might be Crying (1973, Allison & Busby). A Sort of Peace (1973, Allison & Busby). The Prisoner (1974). The Prince and the Tobacco Lords (1976, Allison & Busby). Many short stories for magazines and radio.

18 Botanic Crescent, N. Kelvinside, Glasgow G20 8QJ. 041-945 0648.

Derwent, Lavinia
Born on a Border farm. Began writing for BBC Children's Hour. Now lives and works in Glasgow. Vice-president, Scottish PEN. MBE.

Many children's books. The Macpherson Series. The Sula Books (Gollancz and Piccolo). A Breath of Border Air (1975, Hutchinson). The Adventures of Tammy Troot (1975, Holmes McDougall). The Boy in the Bible (1973, Blackie). Further Adventures of Tammy Troot (1975, Holmes McDougall).

Frequent appearances on television, including cameos of childhood life in the Borders.

1 Great Western Terrace, Glasgow.

Devine, David McDonald (Dominic)
Born Greenock 1920. Educ. Glasgow and London Univs.

My Brother's Killer (1961). Doctors Also Die (1962). The Royston Affair (1964). His Appointed Day (1965). Devil at Your Elbow (1966). Fifth Cord (1967). Sleeping Tiger (1968). Death is My Bridegroom (1969). Illegal Tender (1970). Dead Trouble (1971). Three Green Bottles (1972).

Deyell, Annie
Born Shetland 1898. Bigton School; Aberdeen Coll. of Education. Taught in Shetland until retirement in 1962.

My Shetland (1975, Thuleprint).

Burnside Walls, Shetland ZE2 9PG.

Donald, Henry
The Happy Story of Wallace the Engine (1955, Nelson). The Story of Hal 5 and the Haywards (1955, Nelson). A Bunch of Sweet Peas (1966, BBC Publications).

BBC Radio 1950-72. Short stories, drama criticism, children's serials, talks, schools programmes.

Plays: Carlyle and Jane (1974, Edinburgh Festival). Edwin and Willa Muir (1976, Edinburgh Festival). The View from Eden, a recital in two acts (1976, Edinburgh Festival).

Donaldson, Gordon
Born Edinburgh 1913. Educ. Royal High School, Edinburgh Univ. (D.Litt), London Univ. (Ph.D.). Asst. Keeper General Register House, Edinburgh, 1938-47. Lecturer, Scottish History, Edinburgh Univ., 1947; Reader, 1955. Professor of Scottish History and Palaeography, Edinburgh Univ. since 1963. Member of the Royal Commission on Ancient and Historical Monuments of Scotland; Scottish National Portrait Gallery Advisory Committee. Co-editor *Scottish Historical Review.*

The Making of the Scottish Prayer Book 1637 (1954). Shetland Life under Earl Patrick (1958). Scotland: Church and Nation through sixteen centuries (1960; 2nd edn. 1972). The Scottish Reformation (1960). Scotland: James V to James VII (1964). The Scots Overseas (1966). Northwards by Sea (1966). Scottish Kings (1967). Memoirs of Sir James Melville (1969). The First Trial of Mary, Queen of Scots (1969). Scottish Historical Documents (1970). Who's Who in Scottish History (1973). Mary, Queen of Scots (1974). Scotland:The Shaping of a Nation (1974).

Douglas, Hugh
Born Maybole, Ayrshire, 1928. Educ. George Watson's Coll., Edinburgh. Edinburgh Univ., Aberdeen Univ. 1950-56, editorial staff *The Bulletin*. 1956-60, *The Star*, London. PRO for trade assoc. and consultancy in London. Married, two children. Visiting author Eastern Arts Assoc. writers in schools project.

The Underground Story (1963, Hale). Crossing the Forth (1964, Hale). Careers in Hotel-keeping (1967, Hale). Edinburgh 1968 (Longman Young Books). Burke and Hare, The True Story (1973, Hale). Charles Edward Stewart—the Man, the King, the Legend (1975, Hale). Robert Burns—A Life (1976, Hale).

146 Broadway, Peterborough PE1 4DG. 0733-53006.

Douglas, Ronald Angus MacDonald
Born Edinburgh. "Miseducation in England corrected by a vast experience of life and much foreign travel." Many years actor-manager and director. Founder and director, Inverness Little Theatre. Director of Productions, Olympia Theatre, Dublin. Appeared at Abbey Theatre. Toured with Sir Philip Ben Greet's Shakespearian companies. Played in Sir Nigel Playfair's London productions. Lifelong Scottish nationalist. Hon. Pres. 1320 Club. Director of Club's Foreign Affairs Bureau. Fellow of the Internationaales Institut fur Kunstwissenschaften. Life Member Society of Authors. Life Member Scottish PEN.

Strangers Come Home (Macmillan, New York). The Sword of Freedom (Macmillan NY). The Irish Book (Talbot Press, Dublin; MacMillan, NY). The Scots Book (Chambers, Edinburgh; Macmillan, NY). The Closed Door (Modern Age Books, New York). Scottish Prose Editor, Alba Inserto (Il Bemestre, Milan). Author of Una Breva Storia di Scozia (Il Bemestre, Milan). Editor, English Language Bureau, Strasbourg. Managing editor Catalyst magazine (1971-73), editorial adviser (1973-74). *Plays:* The Red Laugh (New Theatre, Winchester and 18 month tour). The Woman Beyond (Olympia Theatre, Dublin, 1945). Several one-act plays.

Tigh an Uillt, Wilton Dean, by Hawick. 0450 3625.

Drawbell, James
Born Falkirk. Worked on newspapers in New York (*The World*), Montreal (*Star*), Edinburgh (*News*), London (editor *Sunday Chronicle*). Managing editor Newnes (later IPC) women's magazines for 17 years.

The Sun Within Us (Collins). Dorothy Thompson's English Journey (Collins). This Year, Next Year (Collins). Good Time (Collins). Film Lady (Collins). Time on My Hands (Macdonald). Scotland Bitter-sweet (Macdonald). A Garden (Macdonald). The Long Year: 1939-40 (Wingate). Night and Day (Hutchinson). All Change Here (Hutchinson). Drifts My Boat (Hutchinson).

Films: Love Story. Innocents of Chicago. *Play:* Who Goes Next? with Reginald Simpson (1929, Arts Theatre, London).

4 Bradbury, North Berwick, East Lothian.

Drummond, Cherry (Cherry Evans)
Born London 1928. Educ. St Andrews Univ., Cambridge Univ. Married to author and farmer Humphrey Drummond. Six children.

Love from Belinda (1961, Hodder). Lalage in Love (1962, Hodder). Creatures Great and Small (1968, Hodder). Stories and poems in various magazines and on BBC.

Megginch Castle, Errol, Perthshire. Errol 222.

Drummond, Humphrey
Born 1922. Educ. Eton; Trinity Coll., Cambridge. 1940-46, Mountain Regiment. MC. Chairman, Soc. of Authors, Scotland.

Falconry for You (1961, Foyle). Le Grand Duc (1966, Quaritch). Falconry in the East (1967, Quaritch). Our Man in Scotland (1969, Frewin). Falconry, an Illustrated Introduction (1974, Bartholomew). The Queen's Man: Life of Bothwell (1975, Frewin).

Megginch Castle, Errol, Perthshire. Errol 222.

Duncan, Jane
Born Renton, Dunbartonshire 1910. Educ. Lenzie Academy, Glasgow Univ. Served in Air Intelligence (WAAF). After 1945 travel and writing.

The Reachfar series of novels: My Friends the Miss Boyds. My Friend Muriel. My Friend Monica. My Friend Annie. My Friend Sandy. My Friend Martha's Aunt. My Friend Flora. My Friend Madame Zora. My Friend Rose. My Friend Cousin Emmie. My Friends the Mrs Millers. My Friends from Cairnton. My Friend my Father. My Friends the Macleans. My Friends the Hungry Generation. My Friend the Swallow. My Friend Sashie. My Friends the Misses Kindness.

The Jean Robertson quartette: Jean in the Morning. Jean at Noon. Jean in the Twilight. Jean towards Another Day. (Under pseudonym Janet Sandison). *For Young People:* Camerons on the Train. Camerons on the Hills. Camerons at the Castle. Camerons Calling. Camerons Ahoy! *For Small Children:* Herself and Janet Reachfar. *Autobiography:* Letter from Reachfar.
(All books published by Macmillan).

The Old Store, Poyntzfield, by Conon Bridge, Ross-shire IV7 8LU. Poyntzfield 249.

Duncan, Margaret
Born Newcastle-upon-Tyne 1917. Diploma in Fine Art, Dunelm. Art teacher in Northumberland until marriage to a history teacher. Two daughters, one son. Came to Scotland in 1948. Lived in Edinburgh, Fife and the Stewartry before settling in Arran in 1968. Now running handloom weaving business with younger daughter.

The Witch Stone (1975, Weidenfeld).

Rowallan, Whiting Bay, Isle of Arran. 077 07 282.

Dunn, Douglas
Born Inchinnan, Renfrewshire, 1942. Educ. Renfrew High; Camphill School, Paisley; Hull Univ. Freelance writer and journalist since 1971.

Terry Street: Poems (1969, Faber). The Happier Life: Poems (1972, Faber). Love or Nothing: Poems (1974, Faber). Edit. A Choice of Lord Byron's Verse (1974, Faber). Edit. New Poems 1972-73, PEN Anthology (1973, Hutchinson). Edit. Two Decades of Irish Writing (1975, Carcanet).

Broadcasting: Early Every Morning, BBC Schools TV, film with verse, 1975. Talks, anthologies, BBC Third Programme. *Play:* Experience Hotel, verse play with music (1975, Humberside Theatre, Hull).

c/o Faber & Faber Ltd., 3 Queen Square, London WC1N 3AU.

Dunnett, Alastair MacTavish
Born Kilmacolm, 1908. Educ. Overnewton School; Hillhead High, Glasgow. Chairman, Thomson Scottish Petroleum Ltd., 1972- . Member Executive Board The Thomson Organisation Ltd., 1973- . Director Scottish Television, 1975- . Co-founder of the Claymore Press 1933-34. Chief Press Officer to the Secretary of State for Scotland 1940-46. Editor of the *Daily Record* until 1955. Editor of *The Scotsman* 1955-72. Chairman, The Scotsman Publications Ltd., 1970-74. Managing Director *The Scotsman* 1962-70. Member Thomson Regional Newspapers board until 1974. Member Scottish International Education Trust, Scottish International Information Committee. Governor Pitlochry Festival Theatre. Member Council CPU, Edinburgh Festival Society and associated with Scottish Opera and Scottish Theatre Ballet.

Treasure at Sonnach (1935). Heard Tell (1946, Albyn Press). Quest by Canoe (1950).

Highlands and Islands of Scotland (1951, Collins). The Duke's Day, under name of Alec Tavis (1970, Hamilton).
Plays: The Original John Mackay (1956, Citizens Theatre, Glasgow). Fit to Print (1962, Duke of York's, London).
87 Colinton Road, Edinburgh EH10 5DF. 031-337 2107.

Dunnett, Dorothy
Born Dunfermline 1923. Educ. James Gillespie's High School for Girls, Edinburgh. Asst. Press Officer, Public Relations Branch, Scottish Home Dept., Edinburgh. Executive Officer, Board of Trade, Glasgow. Married Alastair M. Dunnett, 1946, two sons. Professional portrait painter since 1950. Member, Board of Trustees, Scottish National War Memorial.
The Game of Kings (1961, Cassell). Queen's Play (1964, Cassell). The Disorderly Knights (1966, Cassell). Dolly and the Singing Bird (1968, Cassell). Pawn in Frankincense (1969, Cassell). Dolly and the Cookie Bird (1970). The Ringed Castle (1971, Cassell). Dolly and the Doctor Bird (1971, Cassell). Dolly and the Starry Bird (1973, Cassell). Checkmate (1975, Cassell). Dolly and the Nanny Bird (1976, Michael Joseph). The Dolly novels appear under the name Dorothy Halliday.
87 Colinton Road, Edinburgh EH10 5DF. 031-337 2107.

Elder, Michael
Born London 1931. Educ. New Park School, St Andrews; Dulwich College, London; Royal Academy of Dramatic Art, London. Worked as actor at Byre Theatre, St Andrews; Citizens' Theatre, Glasgow; Gateway, Edinburgh; Pitlochry Festival Theatre; Royal Lyceum, Edinburgh. Frequent TV appearances, over 1000 radio broadcasts. Director, Edinburgh Film Festival, 1961-63.
Affair at Invergarroch (1951, Black). Tony Behind the Scenes (1955, Murray). Cabin at Bartonbridge (1956, Murray). Phantom in the Wings (1957). For Those in Peril (1963, Murray). The Young Martin Luther (Parrish). The Young James Barrie (Macdonald). Paradise is not Enough (1970, Hale). The Alien Earth (1971, Hale). Nowhere on Earth (1972, Hale). The Everlasting Man (1972, Hale). The Perfumed Planet (1973, Hale). Down to Earth (1973, Hale). A Different World (1974, Hale). Seeds of Frenzy (1974, Hale). Centaurian Quest (1975, Hale). Island of the Dead (1975, Hale). Nearly 200 radio scripts.
20 Zetland Place, Edinburgh EH5 3LY. 031-552 1603.

Eveling, Stanley
Born Newcastle upon Tyne, 1925. Educ. Durham Univ., Oxford.
The Balachites, The Strange Case of Martin Richter (1970, Playscript 20, Calder & Boyars). The Lunatic, the Secret Sportsman and the Women Next Door (1970, Playscript 30, Calder & Boyars). Vibrations; Come and Be Killed; Dear Janet Rosenberg, Dear Mr Kooning (1971, Playscript 37, Calder & Boyars).
Television: A Man Like That (1965). Ishmael (1973).
Radio Plays: Dance ti thy Daddy (1964). The Timepiece (1965). A Man Like That (1966). The Queen's Own (1976).
Plays: The Balachites (1963, Edinburgh Traverse). An Unspeakable Crime (1963, London). Come and Be Killed (1967, Edinburgh; 1968, London). The Strange Case of Martin Richter (1967, Close Theatre, Glasgow; 1968, London). The Lunatic, the Secret Sportsman and the Women Next Door (1968, Traverse, Edinburgh; 1969, London). Dear Janet Rosenberg, Dear Mr Kooning (1969, Traverse, Edinburgh; 1970, London; New York). Vibrations (1969, Edinburgh; 1972, London). Dracula (1969, Edinburgh; 1973, London). Mister (1971, London). Better Days, Better Knights (1971, Edinburgh; 1972, London). Our Sunday Times (1971, Edinburgh; London). Oh Starlings (1971, Edinburgh). Sweet Alice (1971, Edinburgh; 1970, New York). The Laughing Cavalier (1971, London). He Used to Play for Hard Hearts (1971, Edinburgh). Careweggio Buddy (1972, Edinburgh). Unwin Jack and Bonzo (1973, Edinburgh; London). Shivers (1974, London). The Dead of Night (1975, Edinburgh).
30 Comely Bank, Edinburgh EH4 ZAS. 031-332 1905.

Fenton, Alexander
Born 1929. Educ. Drumblade School, Turriff Academy, Aberdeen Univ., Cambridge Univ. Deputy Keeper, National Museum of Antiquities, Edinburgh. Sec., Scottish Country Life Museums Trust.

The Various Names of Shetland (1973, Blackwood). Scottish Country Life (1976, Donald). Edit., with A. Gailey, The Spade in Northern and Atlantic Europe (1970, Ulster Folk Museum). Edit., with J. Podolak, H. Rasmussen, Land Transport in Europe (1973, National Museum, Copenhagen).

National Museum of Antiquities of Scotland, Queen Street, Edinburgh EH2 1JD. 031-556 8921.

Fenwick, Hubert
Born Glasgow 1916. Educ. in New Zealand. Qualified as architect after the War but out of sympathy with modern architecture so concentrated on becoming an architectural historian. Remained on register of Architects in UK and examiner in History and Appreciation for RIBA in Scotland.

Architect Royal, Sir William Bruce (1970, Roundwood Press). The Auld Alliance (1971, Roundwood Press). Scotland's Historic Buildings (1974, Hale). The Chateaux of France (1975, Hale). Scotland's Castles (1976, Hale).

15 Randolph Crescent, Edinburgh 3. 031-225 7982.

Fergusson, Bernard (Brigadier Lord Ballantrae, Kt., GCMG, GCVO, DSO, OBE, D.Litt., DCL, LLD)
Born 1911. Educ. Eton, Sandhurst. Distinguished service in the Middle East, India and Burma, 1939-45. Director Combined Ops., Military, 1945-46. Col. Intelligence, Supreme HQ Allied Powers Europe, 1951-53. Governor General of New Zealand 1962-67.

Eton Portrait (1937). Beyond the Chindwind (1945). Lowland Soldier, Poems (1945). Wild Green Earth (1946). The Black Watch and the King's Enemies (1950). Rupert of the Rhine (1952). The Rare Adventure (1954). The Watery Maze, the Story of Combined Operations (1961). Wavell (1961). Return to Burma (1962). Trumpet in the Hall (1970). Captain John Niven (1972).

Auchairne, Ballantrae, Ayrshire.

Fiddler, Kathleen
Author of many children's books including: The Boy with the Bronze Axe (Puffin). Haki, the Shetland Pony (1968, Lutterworth). Flash the Sheep Dog (Lutterworth). Stories of Old Inns (1973, Epworth). Pirate and Admiral (1974, Lutterworth). The Brydons go Canoeing (1963, Lutterworth). Flodden Field (1971, Lutterworth). The '45 and Culloden (1973, Lutterworth). Mountain Rescue Dog (Lutterworth). Treasure of Ebba (1968, Lutterworth). True Tales of Castles (1969, Lutterworth). Turk, the Border Collie (1975, Lutterworth). Diggers of Lost Treasure (1972, Epworth). Gold of the Castle (1970, Lutterworth).

Janebank, Lasswade, Midlothian.

Findlay, William
Born Culross, Fife, 1947. Educ. Newbattle Abbey, Universities of Stirling, California and Edinburgh. Winner of the McCash Prize in Scots Poetry, 1975.

Parkland Poets No. 12 (1975, Akros).

3 Bridgehaugh Road, Stirling.

Finlay, Ian
Born Auckland, New Zealand, 1906. Educ. Edinburgh Academy, Edinburgh Univ. Joined staff of Royal Scottish Museum 1932. Keeper of Dept. of Art and Ethnography 1956. Director 1961-71. Secretary to Royal Fine Art Commission for Scotland 1953-61. First Chairman Soc. of Authors Scottish Committee. Freeman City of London and Liveryman Worshipful Co. of Goldsmiths. CBE. Amenity Trustee Palace of Holyrood-

house. Former Vice-chairman Scottish Arts Council. Honorary Royal Scottish Academician and Professor of Antiquities.

Scotland (1945, OUP). Scottish Art (1945, Brit. Council). Art in Scotland (1948, OUP). Scottish Crafts (1948, Harrap). Scotland, Young Traveller series (1953, Phoenix). History of Scottish Gold and Silver Work (1956, Chatto). Scotland, enlarged edit. (1957, Chatto). The Lothians (1960, Collins). The Highlands (1963, Batsford). The Lowlands (1967, Batsford). Celtic Art—An Introduction (1973, Faber). In the press: The Central Highlands (Batsford). The Future of Museums (Faber).

Currie Riggs, Balerno, Midlothian. 031-449 4249.

Finlay, Ian Hamilton
Born 1925. Perhaps the best-known concrete poet, uses a variety of materials as well as the printed word. At Stoneypath in Lanarkshire has laid out a unique garden as a setting for his concrete creations. His work was exhibited at the Scottish National Gallery of Modern Art in 1972. Edited Poor Old Tired Horse poetry sheet, issues 1-25. His printed works, in books, booklets, wall sheets and cards are mainly published by the Wild Hawthorn Press.

Ford, James Allan
Born Auchtermuchty 1920. Educ. Royal High School, Edinburgh; Edinburgh Univ. 1940-46, Royal Scots, Captain. Served in Hongkong. Was prisoner of war in Japanese hands 1941-45. Civil servant since 1938. Asst. Secretary, Dept. of Agriculture for Scotland, 1958. Registrar General for Scotland, 1966. Under Secretary, Scottish Office, 1969-   . Pres. Scottish PEN, 1970-73.

Brave White Flag (1961, Hodder). Season of Escape (1963, Hodder). Statue for a Public Place (1965, Hodder). A Judge of Men (1968, Hodder). Mouth of Truth (1972).

29 Lady Road, Edinburgh EH16 5AP.

Fowler, Alastair D. S.
Born 1930. Educ. Queen's Park School, Glasgow; Glasgow Univ.; Edinburgh Univ.; Pembroke Coll., Oxford. Regius Professor of Rhetoric and English Literature, Edinburgh Univ. since 1972. Fellow and Tutor in English Lit., Brasenose Coll., Oxford, 1962-71. Member of Scottish Arts Council, 1976.

Trans., edit., Richard Wills, De re poetica (1958, Blackwell). Spencer and the Numbers of Time (1964, Routledge). Edit., C. S. Lewis, Spencer's Images of Life (1967, CUP). Edit., with John Carey, Poems of John Milton (1968, Longman). Triumphal Forms (1970, CUP). Silent Poetry (1970). Edit., with C. Butler, Topics in Criticism (1971, Longman). Seventeen (Sycamore). Conceitful Thought (1976, Edin.UP). Catacomb Suburb (1976, Edin. UP).

Dept. of English Literature, University of Edinburgh, David Hume Tower, George Square, Edinburgh EH8 9JX. 031-667 1011, Ext. 6259.

Fraser, Amy Stewart
Born Ballater, 1892. Educ. Esdaile Coll., Edinburgh; Dunfermline Coll. of Hygiene and Physical Training. MBE, Coronation Medal, WVS Long Service Medal. After a lifetime of voluntary public service is now retired and enjoys the society of her family, twelve grandchildren and five great-grandchildren. Former Carlisle City Councillor; National Chairman, Electrical Assoc. for Women; Pres., Carlisle branch, NSPCC.

The Hills of Home (1973, Routledge). Dae ye min' Langsyne? (1975, Routledge). Companion book to The Hills of Home to be published in 1977.

Hill Crest House, Harraby Grove, Carlisle CA1 2QN. Carlisle 21423.

Fraser, Douglas
Born Edinburgh 1910. Educ. George Heriot's School, Edinburgh. Retired Insurance Clerk. Married, one daughter, two sons. Committee Member, Scottish PEN. Hon. Treas., Scottish Association for the Speaking of Verse. Hon. Sec. Edinburgh Poetry Club.

Landscape of Delight (1967, Macdonald). Rhymes o' Auld Reekie (1973, Macdonald).

2 Keith Terrace, Edinburgh EH4 3NJ. 031-332 5176.

Fraser, Duncan
Born Glasgow 1905. Educ. Glasgow Univ. FSA Scot. Specialises in illustrated books, most of the photographs being taken by himself; designs the books and prints them at the Standard Press in Montrose.
Land of the Ogilvys (1964). Montrose before 1700 (1967). Highland Perthshire (1969). Portrait of a Parish (1970). The Smugglers (1971). Glen of the Rowan Trees (1973). East Coast Oil Town (1974). Edinburgh in Olden Times (1976). All published by Standard Press, Montrose.
Standard House, Montrose. Montrose 2251.

Fraser, George MacDonald
Born Carlisle 1925. Carlisle Grammar School, Glasgow Academy. Served World War II, infantryman XIVth Army, lieutenant Gordon Highlanders. Newspaperman, England, Canada, Scotland, 1947-69. Deputy Editor, *Glasgow Herald*, 1964-69.
Flashman (1969). Royal Flash (1970). The General Danced at Dawn (1970). Flash for Freedom! (1971). The Steel Bonnets (1971). Flashman at the Charge (1973). McAuslan in the Rough (1974). Flashman in the Great Game (1975). British editions all by Barrie and Jenkins.
Film screenplays: The Three Musketeers (1973). Royal Flash (1975). The Four Musketeers (1975).

Fraser, G. S.
Born 1915.
Poetry: Fatal Landscape (1941). Home Town Elegy (1944). The Traveller has Regrets (1948). Leaves without a Tree (1953). Conditions (1969). *Prose:* The Modern Writer and His World (1953). W. B. Yeats (1954). Scotland (1955). Dylan Thomas (1957). Vision and Rhetoric (1959). Ezra Pound (1960). Lawrence Durrell (1968). Metre, Rhyme and Free Verse (1970).

Fulton, Robin
Born Scotland 1937. Educ. Edinburgh Univ., MA, Ph.D. Schoolteaching in Scotland, 1959-69. Writer's Fellowship, Edinburgh Univ., 1969-71. Now living in Scandinavia. Edit. *Lines Review* 1967-77.
Poetry: Instances (1967, Macdonald). Inventories (1969, Caithness Books). Spaces between the Stones (1971, New Rivers Press, New York). Man with the Surbahar (1971, Macdonald). Tree-Lines (1974, New Rivers Press).
Translations: Italian Quartet (1966, London Mag. Editions). Blok's Twelve (1968, Akros). Five Swedish Poets (1972, Seton Hall Univ., NJ). Lars Gustafsson: Selected Poems (1972, New Rivers Press). Gnnnar Harding: They Killed Sitting Bull (1973, London Mag. Editions). Tomas Tranströmer: Selected Poems (1974, Penguin). Osten Sjostrand: Hidden Music (1975, Oleander Press).
Criticism: Contemporary Scottish Poetry: Individuals and Contexts (1974, Macdonald).

Gallacher, Tom
Born Dunbartonshire 1934. Writer in Residence, Pitlochry Festival Theatre, 1975- .
Plays: Our Kindness to Five Persons (1969, Glasgow). Mr Joyce is Leaving Paris (1971, Dublin; 1972, London). Revival! (1972, Dublin, 1973, London). Three to Play (1972, Montrose). Schellenbrack (1973, London; 1973, Pitlochry). Bright Scene Fading (1973, London; 1975, Glasgow). The Only Street (1973, Dublin; 1973, London; 1974, Ochtertyre). Personal Effects (1974, Pitlochry). A Laughing Matter (1975, St Andrews). Hallowe'en (1975, Dundee). The Sea Change (1976, Edinburgh). A Presbyterian Wooing (1976, Pitlochry). *Radio Plays:* BBC Scotland—The Scar (1974). Hunting Shadows (1975). The Man With a Hatchet (1976).

Gardner, Leslie
Born Stafford, England, 1921. Educ. King Edward VI School, Stafford; Royal Naval Coll., Greenwich. Royal Navy 1939-56. Author and traveller 1960-76.
Stage Coach to John o' Groats (1961, Hollis & Carter). Man in the Clouds (1963,

Chambers). Call the Captain (1964, Blackwood). The Royal Oak Courts Martial (1965, Blackwood). The Eagle Spreads his Claws (1966, Blackwood). The British Admiralty (1968, Blackwood). South to Calabria (1968, Blackwood). Curtain Calls (1976, Duckworth). Iron Filings (1976, Duckworth). *Radio Play:* Three Men in a Battleship (1970).

Bolton Muir Lodge, Gifford, East Lothian.

Garioch, Robert (Robert Garioch Sutherland)

Born Edinburgh 1909. Writer in Residence Edinburgh Univ., 1971-73. Prisoner of war in Italy and Germany. Editorial Adviser, *Scottish International Review*, 1968-74.

Selected Poems (1966, Macdonald). The Big Music (1971, Caithness Books). Doktor Faust in Rose Street (1973, Macdonald). Two Men and a Blanket (1976, Southside).

Garry, Flora

Born New Deer, Aberdeenshire, 1900. Educ. New Deer village school, Peterhead Academy, Aberdeen Univ. Taught English at Dumfries Academy and Strichen Secondary School. Married Robert Campbell Garry, Regius Professor of Physiology, Glasgow Univ. One son.

Bennygoak and Other Poems (1974, Rainbow Books). Bennygoak; cassette (1975, Scotsoun). Poems in various anthologies and on radio.

Laich Dyke, Dalginross, Comrie, Perthshire. Comrie 474.

Gaston, William James (Bill)

Born Glasgow 1927. Educ. Rothesay Academy. Engineering apprentice 1943-48. Currently with Rolls-Royce. Married 1950, one daughter, two sons.

As Bill Gaston: Deep Green Death (1963, Hammond). Drifting Death (1964, Hammond). Death Crag (1965, Hammond). Death Dealers (1967, Hammond). Dark Roots of Fear (1969, Jenkins). Shabby Eagles (1973, Hale). Winter of the Wildcat (1977, Hale).

As Jack Bannantyne: Torpedo Squadron (1975, Hale).

9 Falstaff, East Kilbride, G74 3RL. East Kilbride 24660.

Gayre of Gayre and Nigg, Robert (Lt. Col.)

Educ. Edinburgh Univ., Oxford Univ.; D.Phil., Mersina; D.Pol.Sc., Palermo; D.Sc., Naples. Education Adviser, Allied Military Government, Head of Education, Allied Control Commission, Italy. Chief of Education and Religious Officer, SHAEF, for Germany. Editor, *Mankind Quarterly*; Mankind Monographs. Consultore pro lingua Anglica, Collegio Araldica, Rome. Grand Commander Military and Hospitaller Order of St Lazarus.

Teuton and Slav on the Polish Frontier (1944, Eyre & Spottiswoode). Italy in Transition (1946, Faber). Wassail! in Mazers of Mead (1948, Phillimore). Heraldry of St John (1956, Garga, Allahabad). Ethnological Elements of Africa (1966). More Ethnological Elements of Africa (1972). Miscellaneous Studies Vols I and II (1972). The Knightly Twilight (1973). Syro-Mesopotamian Ethnology as Revealed in Genesis X (1973). The Lost Clan (1974).

Minard Castle, by Inverary, Argyll. Minard 272.

Gerson, Jack

Born Glasgow 1928. Educ. Hillhead High School. Married, one daughter. Served in RAF 1947-49. Won BBC Scotland Play Competition 1959. Has worked in advertising and the cinema industry. Member Scottish Committee PEN, Scottish Committee, Writers Guild.

Man on the Crater's Edge, novel (1972, Hale). The Regiment, novel with Nick McCarty (1973, Pan).

Over 100 television plays and series episodes. Eight radio plays. Co-director with Nick McCarty of BBC series The Regiment.

c/o Harvey Unna and Stephen Burbridge, 14 Beaumont Mews, Marylebone High Street, London W1.

Gibson, John Sibbald
Born Renfrewshire 1923. Educ. Paisley Grammar School, Glasgow Univ. Army 1942-45. Scottish Office, 1947- . Under Secretary since 1973. Married, 1 son, 1 daughter. Interested in Scottish history and writes much on 18th century.
Ships of the '45: the Rescue of the Young Pretender (1967, Hutchinson), adapted for radio by Iain Crichton Smith. Deacon Brodie: Father to Jekyll and Hyde (1977, Paul Harris).
28 Cramond Gardens, Edinburgh EH4 6PY. 031-336 2931.

Gifford, (Thomas) Douglas (MacPharlain)
Born 1940. Educ. Hillhead High School; Glasgow Univ.; Balliol Coll., Oxford.
Edit. Scottish Short Stories 1800-1900 (1971, Calder & Boyars). Edit. James Hogg's Three Perils of Man (1972, Scot. Academic Press). Edit., with Alex. Scott, Neil M. Gunn, the Man and the Writer (1973, Blackwood). James Hogg, New Assessments (1976, Ramsay Head Press).
Has contributed to several radio programmes and series on Scottish writing; regular reviews and broadcasts on the arts in Scotland.
Dept. of English Studies, University of Strathclyde, Glasgow.

Gillies, Valerie
Born 1948. Educ. Edinburgh Univ. Commonwealth Scholar in India. Returned to Scotland to train as an English teacher. Married.
Trio: New Poets from Edinburgh (New Rivers Press). Poetry Introductions 3 (Faber).

Glen, Duncan
Born Cambuslang 1933. Educ. West Coats School, Cambuslang, Rutherglen Academy, Edinburgh Coll. of Art. Worked as typographer and publisher's editor. Currently Head of Graphic Design Division, Preston Polytechnic. Special Award from Scottish Arts Council for services to Scottish Literature, 1975. Director, with Margaret Glen, Akros Publications. Editor *Akros* magazine 1965- .
Hugh MacDiarmid: Rebel Poet and Prophet (1962, Drumalban Press). Hugh Mac-Diarmid and the Scottish Renaissance (1964, Chambers). The Literary Masks of Hugh MacDiarmid (1964, Drumalban Press). Stanes: A Twalsome of Poems (1966, The Author). Scottish Poetry Now (1966, Akros). Idols: When Alexander our King was Dead: Poem (1967, Akros). Edit. Poems Addressed to Hugh MacDiarmid (1967, Akros). Kythings and Other Poems (1969, Caithness Books). Sunny Summer Sunday Afternoon in the Park? (1969, Akros). Edit. Selected Essays of Hugh MacDiarmid (1969, Cape). Unnerneath the Bed: Poem (1970, Akros). Edit. The Akros Anthology of Scottish Poetry 1965-70 (1970, Akros). A Small Press and Hugh MacDiarmid (1970, Akros). The MacDiarmids: A Conversation, with Hugh MacDiarmid (1970, Akros). In Appearances: A Sequence of Poems (1971, Akros). Clydesdale: A Sequence of Peems (1971, Akros). Edit. Whither Scotland? (1971, Gollancz). The Individual and the Twentieth-Century Scottish Literary Tradition (1971, Akros). Feres: Poems (1971, Akros). Edit. Hugh MacDiarmid: A Critical Survey (1972, Scot. Academic Press). A Journey Past: A Poem (1972, privately printed). A Cled Score: Poems (1974, Akros). Compiler, A Bibliography of Scottish Poets from Stevenson to 1974 (1974, Akros). Mr & Mrs J. L. Stoddart at Home: A Poem (1975, Akros). Graphic Lines: magazine (1975). The New Buildings of Preston, with John Brook (1975, Harris Press). Buits and Wellies: Poems (1975, The Author). Edit. with Nat Scammacca, Scottish Poetry for Sicily (1976, Celebes).
Compiler of programmes on Hugh MacDiarmid and Scottish Poetry for BBC. Poetry broadcast on BBC 3 and BBC Scotland.
14 Parklands Avenue, Penwortham, Preston PR1 0QL. Preston 428837.

Gordon, Anne Wolrige
Born London 1936. Educ. Ancaster House, Sussex. Daughter of the late Peter Howard. Married Patrick Wolrige Gordon, one son, two daughters.
Peter Howard, Life and Letters (1968, Hodder). Blindsight (1970, Westminster). Dame Flora (1974, Hodder). *Play:* Blindsight (Westminster Theatre, London).

Gordon, Esme
Born Edinburgh 1910. Educ. Edinburgh Academy; School of Architecture, Edinburgh Coll. of Art. RIBA Owen James Scholarship, 1939. War service RE in Europe. Pres. Edinburgh Architectural Assoc. 1955-57. Member of Scottish Comm. Arts Council of GB 1959-65. ARSA 1956. RSA 1967. Hon. Sec. RSA 1972- .

Short History of St Giles Cathedral (1954, Pillans & Wilson). Principles of Church Building, Furnishing etc. (1963, Church of Scotland). The Royal Scottish Academy 1826-1976 (1976, Skilton).

Gordon, Giles
Born Edinburgh 1940. Educ. Edinburgh Academy. Married Margaret Anna Eastoe—illus. children's books, including the Wombles. Three children. Studied book design and typography at Edinburgh Coll. of Art, then worked as publishing trainee with Oliver & Boyd. 1962-64, advertising manager, Secker & Warburg. 1964-66, editor, Hutchinson. 1966-68, editor Penguin. 1968-72, editorial director, Gollancz. In 1972 became director of literary agents, Anthony Sheil Associates. Was C. Day Lewis fellow in writing, King's Coll., London Univ., 1974-75. Member Literature Panel, Arts Council of GB, 1966-70.

Fiction: Pictures from an Exhibition (1970, Allison & Busby). Umbrella Man (1971, A & B). About a Marriage (1972, A & B). Girl with Red Hair (1974, Hutchinson). Farewell Fond Dreams (1975, Hutchinson). 100 Scenes from Married Life (1976, Hutchinson). *Poetry:* Landscape any Date (1963, Macdonald). Two and Two Make One (1966, Akros). Two Elegies (1968, Turret). Eight Poems for Gareth (1970, Sceptre). Twelve Poems for Callum (1972, Akros). Two Women, One Man (1974, Sheep Press). Edited, with Alex Hamilton, Factions (1974, Joseph). Beyond the Words (1975, Hutchinson). With B. S. Johnson and M. Bakewell, You Always Remember the First Time (1975, Quartet). With D. Barber, Members of the Jury (1976, Wildwood). Prevailing Spirits, A Book of Scottish Ghost Stories (1976, Hamilton). A Book of Contemporary Nightmares (1976, Joseph). For children, with Margaret Gordon, Walter and the Balloon (1974, Heinemann). Poems and short stories in various anthologies. Three radio plays on BBC.

9 St Ann's Gardens, London NW5 4ER. 01-836 8376.

Graham, William
Born Carluke 1913. Educ. Wishaw High School, Glasgow Univ. Has been organist, teacher, airman, nurseryman, shopkeeper, teacher again, and author. Past pres. Ayr Burns Club. Member of comm. Scots Language Soc. Won £1000 first prize in D. C. Thomson's serial story competition 1974. Has since been writing serials under nom-de-plume. Engaged in compiling Scots-English dictionary.

Poetry: That Ye Inherit (1968). Two Three Sangs and Stories (1975).

48 Mount Charles Crescent, Alloway, Ayr. Alloway 43701.

Graham, W. S.
Born Greenock 1918. Gave up engineering to become a writer. Has lived for over twenty years in Cornwall.

Cage Without Grievance (1942). Seven Journeys (1944). Second Poems (1945). White Threshold (1949). The Nightfishing (1955). Malcolm Mooney's Land (1970, Faber).

Grant, I. F.
Born Edinburgh 1887. MBE, LLD. Founder of Highland Folk Museum, Kingussie.

Everyday Life on an Old Highland Farm (1922, Longman). Social and Economic Development of Scotland before 1603 (1929, Oliver & Boyd). Lordship of the Isles (1935, Moray Press). In the Tracks of Montrose (1931). Everyday Life in Old Scotland (1933). Social and Economic History of Scotland (1934). Highland Folk Ways (1961, Routledge). Angus Og of the Isles (1969).

91

Grant, John
Born Edinburgh 1930. George Watson's, Edinburgh, College of Art, Heriot-Watt Univ. Studied Architecture, but gave up practice to lecture and research in Building Technology. Married, with four children. Does book illustration and Television graphics.

Littlenose (1968, BBC Publications). Littlenose Moves House (1969, BBC Publications). Littlenose the Hero (1971, BBC Publications). Littlenose the Hunter (1972, BBC Publications). Littlenose the Fisherman (1974, BBC Publications). Littlenose to the Rescue (1975, BBC Publications). Adventures of Littlenose (collection) (1972, BBC Publications). More Adventures of Littlenose (collection) (1976, BBC Publications).

All above adapted and illustrated for BBC Jackanory. Rullion Green—12 part serial for Radio Forth.

13 Riselaw Road, Edinburgh EH10 6HR. 031-447 3468

Graves, Charles
Born Warwick 1892. Educ. Warwick School. On staffs successively of *Leamington Spa Courier*, *Glasgow Citizen* and *The Scotsman*. Member of the Scottish Comm. of Arts Council for six years. Past pres., Scottish Arts Club. Vice-chairman, Scottish Assoc. for Speaking of Verse.

The Bamboo Grove (1925, Cape). The Wood of Time (1938, Bodley Head). Votive Sonnets (1965, privately). Emblems of Love and War (1970, Ramsay Head Press). Collected Poems (1972, Ramsay Head Press). The Warming Pan (1975, Ramsay Head Press). Trans. Lyrics of Ronsard (1967, Oliver & Boyd).

34 Buckingham Terrace, Edinburgh EH4 3AF.

Green, J. C. R.
Born Glasgow 1949. John Neilson, Paisley and Coimbra University, Portugal. Married, no children. Director Birmingham Poetry Centre 1971: Editor *Muse* magazine 1971-72; Editor Poetry News 1971-72; Chairman Birmingham Poetry Centre 1971-72; Organiser Birmingham & Midland Poetry Festival 1972; Member Birmingham & Midland Institute Council 1972. Producer and Introducer BBC Radio 1972-74; Director Aquila Publishing Co. Ltd. 1972 onwards (publisher Aquila Publishing 1968-72); Editor *Prospice* magazine 1973 onwards; Editor Association of Little Presses Magazine 1973-74; Committee Member Association of Little Presses 1973-74; General Manager Independent Book Dist. 1974 onwards: Director Poetry Roundabout Ltd. 1974 onwards; Editor New Poetry News 1975 onwards.

Go Dig Your Own Grave (poems) (1968, Aertis, USA). Lagos (prose and poetry) (1970, Di Silva, Portugal). Into The Darkness (poems) (1971, Johnston). Trans. Lisbon Revisited (1973, Insight). By Weight of Reason (poems and translations) (1974, Aquila/Phaethon Press). Trans. The Tobacconist (1975, Aquila/Phaethon Press). Trans. Modern Brazilian Poetry (1975, Aquila/Phaethon Press).

Appeared on several TV programmes, and many radio programmes for BBC. Poems and translations on the World Service, also long translation of the poetry of Fernando Pessoa on Portuguese Radio.

"Caladh-na-Sith," Scullamus, Breakish, Isle of Skye IV42 8QB

Grimble, Ian
Ph.D. Aberdeen Univ. Joined BBC from House of Commons Library, 1955, moved to Glasgow in 1957 and to Aberdeen in 1958, where he set up first VHF broadcasting stations in Orkney and the north of Scotland. His historical programmes for BBC TV include: Who are the Scots; Kings, Lords and Commoners and The Scottish Nation.

Books include: The Trial of Patrick Sellar; Chief of Mackay; The Future of the Highlands and Scottish Clans and Tartans.

Haldane, A. R. B.
Born Edinburgh 1900. Educ. Edinburgh Academy; Winchester; Balliol Coll., Oxford. Writer to the Signet. Retired 1970. Farmer and landowner. Trustee, National Library of Scotland.

By Many Waters (1940, Nelson). Path by the Water (1944, Nelson). Drove Roads of Scotland (1951, Nelson). New Ways Through the Glens (1962, Nelson). Three Centuries of Scottish Ports (1971, Edin. Univ. Press). By River, Stream and Loch (1973, David & Charles).

Foswell, Auchterarder. Auchterarder 2610.

Hamilton, Alex.
Born Glasgow 1949. Active in song-writing and performing, tape recording, Scottish Arts Council Writers in Schools Scheme.

Three Glasgow Writers, with Tom Leonard and James Kelman (1976, Molendinar Press). Edit. Scottish Writing (1976, Molendinar Press). Obbligato (1976, Maclellan-Embryo).

1 Westbank Quadrant, Glasgow G12 8NT. 041-339 8444.

Hamilton, Iain (Bertram)
Born 1920. Educ. Paisley Grammar School. Editorial Staff: *Daily Record* 1944-45; *The Guardian* 1945-52; *Spectator* 1952; Asst. Editor 1953, Assoc. Editor 1954-56, *Spectator* Editor-in-Chief 1957; Editorial Director, Hutchinson group, 1958-62; Editor of *Spectator* 1962-63.

Founder and Executive Member, British Irish Association.

Scotland the Brave (1957). The Foster Gang with H. J. May (1966). Embarkation for Cythera (1974).

Play: The Snarling Beggar (1951, Rutherglen Repertory Theatre).

31 Highgate West Hill, London N.6 and Kames, Tighnabruaich, Argyll.

Hanley, Clifford
Born Glasgow 1922. Educ. Eastbank Academy, Glasgow. Journalist, 1940-60, *News of the World*, *Scottish Daily Record*, *TV Guide*, Glasgow *Evening Citizen*. Freelance writer 1960- . Member Scottish Arts Council 1968-75; Scottish chairman, Writers Guild 1966-72; Member governing board Third Eye arts centre 1974- ; Scottish president International PEN 1974- .

Dancing in the Streets (1958). Love from Everybody (1959). Taste of Too Much (1959). Nothing but the Best (1964). Skinful of Scotch (1965). The Hot Month (1967). Red-haired Bitch (1969). (All Hutchinson). Under pseudonym Henry Calvin: The System (1962). It's Different Abroad (1963). Italian Gadget (1966). A Nice Friendly Town (1967). DNA Business (1967). Miranda Must Die (1968). The Chosen Instrument (1969). The Poison Chasers (1971). Take Two Popes (1972). (All Hutchinson).

Innumerable contributions to Radio and TV features.

Plays: The Durable Element (1960, Dundee Rep.). Saturmacnalia (1961, Glasgow Citizens). Oh for an Island (1962, Glasgow). Dick McWhittie (1963, Glasgow). Oh Glorious Jubilee (1971, Leeds Playhouse).

36 Munro Road, Glasgow.

Hardie, George
Born Hamilton 1933. Educ. Hamilton Academy. Married 1960. Quantity Surveyor. Forced furth o' Scotland by unemployment 1971. Active member SNP 1950-71 and still an ardent nationalist. SNP Member of Hamilton Town Council 1967-70. Founder Editor (with Walter Perrie) of *The Chapman* 1970-71.

Poetry: Voice of the Curlew (1966, Privately). Poems (1969, Akros).

Balldown Farmhouse, Sparsholt, nr Winchester, Hants. Sparsholt 553.

Hardy, H. Forsyth
Born Bathgate 1910. Educ. Bathgate Academy. On staff of *The Scotsman*, 1930-41; first film critic. Chief Press Officer, Scottish Information Office, 1941-55. Director, Films of Scotland, 1955-75. Chairman, Arts Review (BBC Scotland) 1950-70. Office-bearer, Edinburgh Film Guild, 1930-75. Secretary, Federation of Scottish Film Societies, 1934-56. Hon. Vice-president, Edinburgh Film Festival.

Grierson on Documentary (1946, Collins; 1966, Faber). Filmgoers' Review (1945, 1946, 1947. Albyn Press). Twenty Years of British Film (part author) (1947, Falcon Press). Scandinavian Film (1952, Falcon Press; 1972, Arno Press). Biography of John Grierson (in preparation).
Mirror of Scotland, BBC TV. Contributor to The Arts in Scotland (BBC Scotland). Film treatments: Lothian Landscape. Shetland: The Sea Around Us. Outline treatment, The Duna Bull.
14 Greenhill Gardens, Edinburgh EH10 4BW. 031-447 4422.

Harris, Paul
Born Barnhurst 1948. Educ. Elgin Academy, Aberdeen Univ. Chairman Scottish General Publishers Association. Committee Member International PEN (Scotland) and the Society of Authors.
When Pirates Ruled the Waves (1968, Impulse). The Garvie Trial (1969, Impulse). To Be A Pirate King (1971, Impulse). Oil (1975, Muller). Le Quatoeur Infernal (1975, Les Presses de la Cite). A Concise Dictionary of Scottish Painters (1976, Paul Harris Publishing).
25 London Street, Edinburgh EH3 6LY. 031-556 9696.

Hay, George Campbell
Born 1915, son of J. MacDougall Hay, author of Gillespie. Brought up in Argyll. War service in North Africa. Notable Gaelic scholar and poet.
Fuaran Sleibh (1947). O Na Ceithir Airdean (1952). Wind on Loch Fyne (1948). Four Points of a Saltire, with others (1970, Reprographia).

Haynes, Dorothy K.
Born Lanark 1918. Educ. Lanark Grammar School; St Margaret's, Aberlour. Married, two sons. Member Lanark Town Council, 1972-75.
Winter's Traces (1947, Methuen). Robin Ritchie (1949, Methuen). Thou Shalt Not Suffer a Witch: short stories (1949, Methuen). Haste Ye Back: autobiography (1973, Jarrolds). Short stories in various anthologies. Over fifty stories broadcast. Winner of Tom Gallon Award, 1947.
14 Quarryknowe, Lanark ML11 7AH. Lanark 3834.

Henderson, Hamish
Born Blairgowrie 1919. Educ. Blairgowrie High School; Dulwich Coll.; Downing Coll., Cambridge. War service, Middle East, Italy, 1940-45. District Sec., WEA, Belfast, 1947-49. Italy, translating Gramsci, 1950. Senior Lecturer, School of Scottish Studies, Edinburgh Univ.
Ballads of World War II (1947, privately for Lili Marlene Club, Glasgow). Elegies for the Dead in Cyrenaica (1948, Lehmann). Trans. Antonio Cramsci's Letters from Prison (1974, EUSPB).
20 Melville Terrace, Edinburgh EH9 1LY. 031-667 5143.

Hendry, J. F.
Born 1912.
Poetry: Bombed Happiness (1942). Orchestral Mountain (1943). *Prose:* Blackbird of Ospo (1945). Fernie Brae: a Scottish Childhood (1947). Verlon and the New Image (1965). Edit. Scottish Short Stories (1970, Penguin).

Herdman, John
Born Edinburgh 1941. Educ. Merchiston Castle, Edinburgh; Magdalene Coll., Cambridge. Read English at Cambridge and later did research in Scottish literature. After a restless few years has lived in Edinburgh, since 1967. Helps organise poetry readings with The Heretics.
Descent: fiction-essay (1968, Fiery Star Press). A Truth Lover: novel (1973, Akros). Memoirs of My Aunt Minnie: short stories (1974, Rainbow Books).
Flat 19, 2 Pentland Drive, Edinburgh EH10 6PX. 031-445 2414.

Highlands, Alexander
The Dark Horizon (1971, Jarrold).

Hignett, Sean
Born Birkenhead 1934. Educ. Birkenhead School; St Peter's Coll., Oxford.
A Picture to Hang on the Wall (1966, Joseph). A Cut Loaf (1971, Joseph). *Plays:* Jack of Spades (1965, Everyman, Liverpool). Allotment (1973, Pool Theatre, Edinburgh). And Did He Come? (Traverse Theatre, Edinburgh). Numerous TV scripts.
Brunstane House, Edinburgh 15.

Hill, C. W.
Born Staffordshire 1915. Educ. Wolverhampton Grammar School. Royal Navy 1941-48. Tutor in History, Wulfrun College of Further Education, Wolverhampton, 1956-68.
Discovering British Postage Stamps (1970, Shire Publications). Discovering Picture Postcards (1970, Shire Publications). Joseph Chamberlain (1973, Shire Publications). Scotland in Stamps (1972, Impulse Books). Edwardian Scotland (1976, Scottish Academic Press).
Regular columns in: *The Observer, Antiquarian Book Monthly Review, Stamp Magazine, Monthly, Look and Learn, Picture Postcard Gazette, Linn's Stamp News* (USA).
Highfield Road, Buckie, Banffshire. Buckie 31158.

Hill, Pamela
Born Nairobi, Kenya, 1920. Hutchesons' Girls' Grammar School, Glasgow; Glasgow School of Art; Glasgow Univ. Taught art intermittently and also sold pottery and bred poodles and tutored biology until "thankfully able to write full time."
Flaming Janet (1954, Chatto). Shadow of Palaces (1955, Chatto). Marjorie of Scotland (1956, Chatto). Here Lies Margot (1957, Chatto). Maddalena (1966, Cassell). Forget Not Ariadne (1967, Cassell). Julia (1968, Cassell). The Devil of Aske (1970, Hodder). The Malvie Inheritance (1971, Hodder). The Incumbent (1972, Hodder). Whitton's Folly (1973, Hodder).
Moorcroft of Glenturp, Newton Stewart, Galloway DG8 9TH. Wigtown 2277.

Hind, Archie
Born Glasgow 1928. Novelist and playwright. Writer in Residence to the community in Aberdeen.
The Deer Green Place (1966, Hutchinson).

House, Jack
Born 1906. Left school at age of fifteen. Trained as a CA "but saw the light." Became a newspaperman in 1928. Worked on all three Glasgow evening papers except for the war years when he was a corporal in the Gordon Highlanders and then captain (scenario editor), Army Kinematograph Service. Vice-chairman, Scottish branch Soc. of Authors.
Down the Clyde (1959, Chambers). Scotland for Fun (1960, Hutchinson). Square Mile of Murder (1961, Chambers). The Heart of Glasgow (1964, Hutchinson). Pavement in the Sun (1967, Hutchinson). Portrait of the Clyde (1969, Hale). Glasgow Old and New (1974, EP Pub.). Also some forty centenary, guide and other publications. Many appearances on TV and radio. For 22 years was one half of the Scottish Round Britain Quiz team.
7 Beaumont Gate, Glasgow G12.

Hunter, Mollie
Born Longniddry, East Lothian. Educ. Preston Lodge School, East Lothian. Married Thomas McIlwraith, two sons. Awards include Scot. Arts Council Literary Award 1972; Child Study Assoc. of America Literary Award 1972; Carnegie Medal 1974; Arbuthnot Honour Lectureship 1975.
Children's books: Patrick Pentigern Keenan (1963, Blackie). Hi Johnny (1963, Evans).

The Kelpie's Pearls (1964, Blackie). The Spanish Letters (1964, Evans). A Pistol in Greenyards (1965, Evans). Ghosts of Glencoe (1966, Evans). Thomas and the Warlock (1967, Blackie). The Ferlie (1968, Blackie). The Lothian Run (1970, Hamilton). The Bodach (1970, Blackie). The Thirteenth Member (1971, Hamilton). Haunted Mountain (1972, Hamilton). The Stronghold (1974, Hamilton). A Stranger Came Ashore (1975, Hamilton). *Other books:* Sound of Chariots (1972, Hamilton). Talent is not Enough (1976, Harper, USA). *Plays:* Love-song for my Lady (1961, Evans). Stay for an Answer (1962, French).
The Sheiling, Milton, by Drumnadrochit, Inverness-shire. Drumnadrochit 267.

Innes, Rosemary Elizabeth (R. E. Jackson)
Born Aboyne, Aberdeenshire. Educ. Howells School, Denbigh; Glasgow School of Art. Was VAD then worked in drawing office during the War. Later qualified as art teacher and taught in Orkney and Aberdeenshire. Married, one daughter.
Witch of Castlekerry (1965, Chatto). The Poltergeist (1968, Chatto). Aunt Eleanor (1969, Chatto, Boyd & Oliver). Ashwood Train (1970, C. B. & O.). Street of Mars (1971, C. B. & O.). Wheel of the Finfolk (1972, Chatto).
Learney, Torphins, Banchory, AB3 4NB. Torphins 228.

Irving, Gordon
Freelance journalist, specialising in theatre. Correspondent for *Variety*, New York, and *The Stage*, London.
Great Scot!, the Story of Harry Lauder (Frewin). The Wit of the Scots (1969, Frewin).

Jackson, Alan
Born 1938.
Poetry: Underwater Wedding (1961). Sixpenny Poems (1962). Well Ye Ken Noo (1963). All Fall Down (1965). The Worstest Beast (1967). Grim Wayfarer (1969). Idiots are Freelance (1973). *Prose:* The Knitted Claymore, an Essay on Culture and Nationalism (1971, *Lines Review*).

Jamieson, Morley
Born Newlandrigg, Midlothian, 1917. Educ. left school at twelve years of age; Newbattle Abbey Coll.; Coleg Harlech, Merioneth.
The Old Wife and Other Stories (1972, Macdonald). Nine Poems (1976, Bruntons). Radio scripts and short stories.
57 West Holmes Gardens, Musselburgh. 031-665 3770.

Jenkins, May Chalmers
Born Knockando, Moray. Educ. Aberdeen Univ. Was a teacher before becoming a journalist in Aberdeen.
Flittings, poetry (1966, Macdonald). Many short stories and poems published and broadcast.
20 Bonnymuir Place, Aberdeen AB2 4NL. 0224 51994.

Jenkins, Robin
Born Cambuslang 1912. Educ. Hamilton Academy, Glasgow Univ. Teacher of English. Happy for the Child (1953). The Thistle and the Grail (1954). The Cone Gatherers (1955). Guests of War (1956). The Missionaries (1957). The Changeling (1958). Some Kind of Grace (1960). Dust on the Paw (1961). Tiger of Gold (1962). A Love of Innocence (1963). Sardana Dancers (1964). A Very Scotch Affair (1968). The Holy Tree (1969). The Expatriates (1971). A Toast to the Lord (1972). A Far Cry from Bowmore (1973). A Figure of Fun (1974).

Johnston, Laughton
Born Aberdeen 1940. Educ. Aberdeen Univ.; Moray House, Edinburgh. Three years Merchant Navy, six years Nature Conservancy Council, responsible for Orkney and Shetland. Resigned in 1975 as senior scientific officer to build home for family.

Poetry: Meetings (1968, Outpost Pubs.). Markland Poets No. 13 (1975, Akros). Several scientific papers.

Little Bousta, Sandness, Shetland ZE2 9PL.

Johnston, Ronald

Born Edinburgh 1926. Educ. Royal High School, Edinburgh; Leith Nautical College. Merchant Navy 1942-47 and 1951-60 (Master Mariner). Life Insurance 1947-51 (Associate of the Chartered Insurance Institute). Cigar Importing 1960-64. Novelist since 1964. Scottish Arts Council 1973-75. Vice-Pres. Scottish PEN. Member Management Comm., Society of Authors 1969-72 and 1975.

Disaster at Dungeness (1964, Collins). Red Sky in the Morning (1965, Collins). The Stowaway (1966, Collins). The Wrecking of Offshore Five (1967, Collins). The Angry Ocean (1968, Collins). The Black Camels of Qashran (1970, Collins). Paradise Smith (1972, Collins). The Eye of the Needle (1975, Collins).

Adaptations and serials of several of above books in papers, magazines and on radio in many countries.

Waverley House, Queen's Crescent, Edinburgh EH9 2BB. 031-667 1282.

Kennedy, Ludovic

Born Edinburgh 1919. Educ. Eton; Christchurch, Oxford. Married Moira Shearer, one son, three daughters. War service in Royal Navy. Atlantic Award in Literature, 1950. Pres., Sir Walter Scott Club, 1968-69. Television editor, presenter, commentator.

Sub-Lieutenant (1942). Nelson's Band of Brothers (1951). One Man's Meat (1953). Ten Rillington Place (1961). Trial of Stephen Ward (1964). Very Lovely People (1969). Story of the Bismark (1974, Collins). Nelson and His Captains (1975, Collins). A Presumption of Innocence (1976, Gollancz).

Play: Murder Story (1954, Cambridge Theatre). *Films:* The Sleeping Ballerina. The Singers and the Songs. Scapa Flow. Battleship Bismark. Scharnhorst.

Makerstoun, Kelso, Roxburghshire. Smailholm 267.

Kincaid, John

Born Glasgow 1909. Educ. Hillhead High School and Jordanhill Training Coll., Glasgow. Married 1930. Insurance clerk 1927-31. Unemployed 1931-33. Credit drapery salesman 1933-35. Tram conductor and driver 1935-41. Dilutee toolroom engineer 1941-43. War service with REME, England, Iraq, Egypt 1943-46. Tram depot handyman 1946-47. Student at Jordanhill 1947-49. Teacher in Glasgow and Shotts, 1949-72. Founder member of Clyde Group, 1943. Executive member Glasgow Unity Theatre 1943 and 1947.

Measures for the Masses: Poems (1943, Maclellan). Time of Violence: Poems (1944, Scoop Books). Setterday Nicht Symphonie (1949, Caledonian Press). Fowrsom Reel: Poems (1930). The Prince (1952, Caledonian Press; Winner of Festival of Britain Long Poem Competition). *Play:* Song of Tomorrow (1943, Glasgow Unity Theatre).

31 Craig Avenue, Whitburn, Bathgate, West Lothian EH47 0NE. Whitburn 40539.

Knight, Alanna

Born Tyneside, of Scots/Irish parents. Educ. Private. Resident in Aberdeen since 1951. Scientist husband, two sons. Comm. of Scottish PEN and Society of Authors; Soc. Women Writers & Journalists; Radiowriters Association; Writers Guild. FSA (Scot.); Lecturer in Creative Writing to WEA, Aberdeen; Founder/Chairman Aberdeen Writers' Circle; Organiser annual "Meet the Author" in Aberdeen; Committee of Aberdeen Arts Centre.

Legend of the Loch (1969, Hurst & Blackett; Netta Muskett Award 1968). The October Witch (1971, Hurst & Blackett). Castle Clodha (1972, Hurst & Blackett). This Outward Angel (1972, Lancer USA). So You Want to Write Pt. 1 (1971, WEA Publications). Lament for Lost Lovers (1972, Hurst & Blackett). The White Rose (1973, Hurst & Blackett). A Stranger Came By (1974, Hurst & Blackett). The Passionate Kindness (1974, Milton House Books). A Drink for the Bridge (1976, Macmillan).

Don Roberto, Radio 4, April 1973—45 minute documentary.

Plays: The Private Life of R. L. Stevenson (1973, Aberdeen Arts Centre; Netherbow Centre, Edin. Fest. Fringe 1973; Young Lyceum, Edin. Fest., 1975).

374 Queen's Road, Aberdeen AB1 8DX. 0224-38388.

Knox, Bill
Born Glasgow 1928. TV and radio drama and documentary script writer and broadcaster. Formerly news editor, STV.

White Water (John Long). Stormtide (John Long). To Kill a Witch (Arrow). Many other crime and adventure stories.

Kyle, Elisabeth
Born Ayr. Educ. privately. First novel published in 1933. Since then has written some forty novels and books for children. Radio plays on Scottish Children's Hour. *Play:* The Singing Wood (1957, Glasgow Citizens).

10 Carrick Park, Ayr. Ayr 63074.

Lamont, Archie
Born Rothesay 1907. Educ. Rothesay Academy, Glasgow Univ. Ph.D.(Glas.), 1935, F.R.S.E., 1950. Lecturer on Stratigraphy, Birmingham University 1936-44. Ecological aspects of Geology and Botany. Hon. Ass. Sec. National Party of Scotland 1928-34.

Education in Scotland (1933, Freeman Pamphlets). Patria Deserta (1943, Oliver & Boyd). Scotland and the War (1943, Scottish Secretariat). Small Nations (1944, Wm. MacLellan). Scotland a Wealthy Country (1945, Scottish Secretariat). How Scotland Lost Her Railways (1947, Scottish Secretariat). Scottish Neutrality (1949, Scottish Secretariat). Sam and Jock the Lallans Cats (1950, Scottish Secretariat). Scotland the Wealthy Nation (1952, Scottish Secretariat). Scotland's Wealth and Poverty (1953, Scottish Secretariat). Buy Scottish Goods (1954, Scottish Secretariat). New Scottish Nationalist Ballads (1974, Scottish Secretariat). How Free is the Scottish Press? (1975, Scottish Secretariat).

Contributor to *Scots Independent* since 1928.

Leonard, Tom
Born Glasgow 1944.

Six Glasgow Poems (1969, Midnight Press). A Priest came to Merkland Street (1970, Midnight Press). Poems (1973, O'Brien, Dublin). Bunnit Husslin (1975, Third Eye, Glasgow). Included in Three Glasgow Writers (1976, Molendinar Press).

56 Eldon Street, Glasgow G3 6NJ.

Lindsay, Frederic
Born Glasgow. Educ. Glasgow Univ., Edinburgh Univ. Has been a research librarian and a schoolmaster. Presently lecturer in English Dept., Hamilton Coll. of Education.

And be the Nation Again: Poems (1975, Akros).

2 Viewpark Drive, Burnside, Rutherglen, Glasgow G73 3QD.

Lindsay, Maurice
Born Glasgow 1918. Educ. Glasgow Academy, Scottish National Academy of Music. Son of Matthew Lindsay and Eileen Frances Brock; married Aileen Joyce Gordon, 1946; three daughters and one son; *Scottish Daily Mail*, drama critic 1946-47; *Bulletin*, Glasgow, music critic 1946-60; BBC Glasgow freelance broadcaster, 1946-61; Border TV, programme controller 1961-62; Production Controller 1962-64; Senior Interviewer and Features Executive 1964-67; 1967—Director of The Scottish Civic Trust. Member of Merchants' House of Glasgow; Fellow of Royal Society of Arts; Life Member of Saltire Society. Founder/co-editor and introducer Scottish Life and Letters (Radio); founder and co-editor and co-introducer Counterpoint (BBC TV Scotland). Involved in producing and presenting many TV programmes.

Poetry: No Crown for Laughter (1943, Fortune Press). The Enemies of Love (1946,

McLellan). Hurlygush (1948, Serif Books). At the Wood's Edge (1950, Serif Books). Ode for St Andrew's Night and other poems (1951, New Alliance Press). The Exiled Heart (1957, Hale). Snow Warning (1962, Linden Press). One Later Day (1964, Brookside Press). This Business of Living (1971, Akros). Comings and Goings (1971, Akros). Selected Poems, 1942-72 (1973, Hale).

Prose: The Scottish Renaissance (1950, Serif Books). The Lowlands of Scotland—Glasgow and the North (1953, Hale; revised edition 1973). Robert Burns: The Man, His Work, the Legend (1954, McGibbon & Kee; revised edition, 1968). The Lowlands of Scotland: Edinburgh and the South (1965, Hale; revised edition 1976). Clyde Waters (1958, Hale). The Burns Encyclopedia (1948, Hutchinson; enlarged and revised edition, 1970). By Yon Bonnie Banks (1962, Hutchinson). The Discovery of Scotland (1964, Hale). The Eye is Delighted—Some Romantic Travellers in Scotland (1971, Muller). Portrait of Glasgow (1972, Hale).

Editor: Sailing Tomorrow's Seas (1944, Fortune Press). Poetry Scotland—4 volumes (1954-53, Vols I-III MacLellan; Vol IV Serif Books). Modern Scottish Poetry (an anthology of the Scottish Renaissance 1920-75) (1946 and 1967, Faber; 1976 Carcanet Press). No Scottish Twilight (with Fred Urquhart) (1947, McLellan). Scottish Poetry (1-6) (with Edwin Morgan and George Bruce))(1966-72, Edin. Univ. Press). Scottish Poetry 7 (with Alexander Scott and Roderick Watson) (1974, Glasgow Univ. Press). Scottish Poetry 8 (with Alexander Scott and Roderick Watson) (1976, Carcanet Press). Scotland—an Anthology (1974, Hale).

Lingard, Joan
Born Edinburgh. Brought up and educ. in Belfast from age 2 to 18. Taught in schools in Belfast, Edinburgh and Midlothian. Now full time writer.
Liam's Daughter (1963). The Prevailing Wind (1964). The Tide Comes In (1966). The Headmaster (1976). A Sort of Freedom (1969). The Lord on our Side (1970). (All Hodder). The Twelfth of July (1970). Across the Barricades (1972). Into Exile (1973). A Proper Place (1975). Frying as Usual (1971). The Clearance (1974). The Resettling (1975). (All Hamilton). Plays for STV and BBC Scotland, serials for STV, scripts for BBC TV Schools.

Lochhead, Liz
Born Motherwell 1947. Educ. Dalziel High School, Motherwell; Glasgow School of Art.
Memo for Spring (1972, Reprographia). Made in Scotland (1974, Carcanet Press). Poetry in various anthologies.
c/o 27 Hamilton Drive, Glasgow G12. 041-339 2711.

Lochhead, Marion Cleland
Born Wishaw 1902. Educ. Glasgow Univ. Moved to Edinburgh 1950. MBE, FRSL.
Poems (1928, Gowans & Gray). Painted Things and Other Poems (1929, Gowans & Gray). Anne Dalrymple (1934). Cloaked in Scarlet (1935). Adrian was a Priest (1936). Island Destiny (1936). Dancing Flower (1937). (All Moray Press). Feast of Candlemass: Poems (1937, Moray Press). Highland Scene (1939, John Smith, Glasgow). On Tintock Tap: Stories for Children (1946, Moray Press). St Mungo's Bairns (1947, Moray Press). The Scots Household in 18th Century (1948, Moray Press, now Chambers). John Gibson Lockhart (1954). Their First Ten Years (1956). Young Victorians (1959). Elizabeth Rigby (1961). Victorian Household (1964). Episcopal Church in 19th Century (1966). (All Murray). Portrait of the Scott Country (1968, Hale).
3 Hope Park Crescent, Edinburgh EH8 9NA. 031-667 8808.

Lomax, E. S.
Born Edinburgh 1919. Educ. Royal High School, Edinburgh; Royal Coll. of Science, Glasgow. 1939-49 British Army, Indian Army. 1949-55 Colonial Admin. Service, Gold Coast. 1957-59 Scot. Gas Board, Edinburgh. 1959-   Lecturer in Personnel Management, Strathclyde Univ.
History of the Volta River Project (1953, Gold Coast Gov.). Transport in Northern

Territories of Gold Coast (1953, Gold Coast Gov.). Intro. Guide to Personnel Selection (1964, Lomax). Human Factors in Communication (1967, Bridgewater Press). Management of Human Resources (1971, BPC). Weekly articles on careers in *The Scotsman*.
21 Heriot Row, Edinburgh EH3 6EN. 031-225 4271.

MacArthur, Bessie Jane Bird
Born Duns, Berwickshire, 1889. Educ. Charlotte Square Inst. and St George's, Edinburgh. Married sheep farmer in Upper Clydeside, 3 sons, 1 daughter. Two sons lost in World War Two. LRAM (Piano).
Clan of Lochlan (1928, Urquhart, Edinburgh). Starry Venture (1930, Elkin Mathews). Scots Poems (1938, Oliver & Boyd). Last Leave (1943, Oliver & Boyd). From Daer Water (1962, Macpherson, Dunfermline). And Time Moves On (1972, Castlelaw Press). Clan of Lochlan was winning play in Scots Radio Drama Competition, 1927; twice televised. Poems in various anthologies.
4 Glencairn Crescent, Edinburgh. 031-225 7418.

Macaulay, Donald (Domhnall MacAmhlaigh)
Born Isle of Lewis 1930. Educ. Nicolson Inst., Stornoway; Aberdeen Univ.; Cambridge Univ. Taught English language in Edinburgh Univ.; Irish in Trinity College, Dublin; Linguistics in Edinburgh. Head of Dept. of Celtic, Aberdeen Univ.
Seobhrach as a' Chlaich, poems (1967, Gairm). Nua-bhardachd Ghaidhlig, bilingual anthology of modern Gaelic poems, with intro. (1976, Canongate).
106 North Deeside Road, Peterculter, Aberdeen AB1 0QB. 0224-732217.

McBain, Hugh
Born Glasgow 1920. Educ. Allan Glen's, St Andrew Univ. 1941-45, Sapper and Sgt. Instructor RAEC. 1937-41 Apprentice engineer. 1948- teacher and lecturer, further education. Member Composers Guild, PEN, Writers Guild.
The Undiscovered Country: Novel (1964, World Distributors). *Play:* In a Class of Her Own (1974). Radio features, stories, talks.
72 Novar Drive, Glasgow G12 9TZ. 041-339 6906.

Macbeth, George
Born 1932. Educ. New Coll. Oxford. Joined BBC 1955. Radio talks and documentary producer. Editor *Poetry Now*, 1965- .
A Form of Words (1954). Broken Places (1963). Doomsday Book (1965). Colour of the Blood (1967). Night of the Stones (1968). War Quartet (1969). The Burning Cone (1970). Collected Poems, 1958-71 (1971). The Orlando Poems (1971). Shrapnel (1972). My Scotland (1973). Macmillan.
BBC, Broadcasting House, London W1A 1AA.

MacCaig, Norman
Born Edinburgh 1910. Educ. Royal High School, Edinburgh; Univ. of Edinburgh. Married, two children. School teacher. Fellow in Creative Writing, Edinburgh Univ. 1967-69. Reader in Poetry, Stirling Univ.
Poetry: Far Cry (1943, Routledge). The Inward Eye (1946, Routledge). Riding Lights (1955, Hogarth). The Sinai Sort (1957, Hogarth). A Common Grace (1960, Hogarth). A Round of Applause (1962, Hogarth). Measures (1965, Hogarth). Surroundings (1966, Hogarth). Rings on a Tree (1968, Hogarth). A Man in My Position (1969, Hogarth). The White Bird (1973, Hogarth). The World's Rooms (1974, Hogarth). Selected Poems (1971, Hogarth). Selected Poems (1972, Penguin). *Edited:* Honour'd Shade (1959, Chambers). Contemporary Scottish Verse (with Alex. Scott) (1970, Calder). For Sydney Goodsir Smith (1975, Macdonald).
7 Leamington Terrace, Edinburgh. 031-229 1809.

McCallum, Neil
Born Portobello 1916. Educ. George Watson's Coll., Edinburgh Univ. Journalist; wartime soldier, North Africa and Sicily; on staff of army newspapers, Italy; advertising

consultant; British representative (1952) at Henry Kissinger's International Seminar, Harvard, USA; Newbattle Abbey Coll.; formerly hon. sec. Edwin Muir Memorial Fund. Member of PEN, Soc. of Authors; past chairman Edinburgh Publicity Club; Pres. Edinburgh Press Club; Fellow Inst. of Practitioners in Advertising; Member Institute of Public Relations.

Half Way House (1949, Cassell). My Enemies Have Sweet Voices (1951, Cassell). It's an Old Scottish Custom (1951, Dobson). Fountainfoot (1952, Cassell). Journey With a Pistol (1959, Gollancz). A Scream in the Sky (1964, Cassell).

Scottish corr., *New Statesman* (1947-52). Stories/poems included in Modern Reading, Penguin Book of Scottish Short Stories, etc.

c/o Scottish Arts Club, 24 Rutland Square, Edinburgh 1.

McCrone, Guy
Born Birkenhead 1898, of Scottish parents. Educ. Glasgow Academy; Pembroke Coll., Cambridge. Sang leading tenor in Erik Chisholm's Trojans, 1936. On boards of Glasgow Chamber Music Soc. and pre-war Scottish Orchestra, Citizens Theatre. Scot. Arts Council for three years.

The Striped Umbrella (1933, Constable). Wax Fruit (1947, Constable). Aunt Bel (1949, Constable). James and Charlott (1953, Constable. Radio, TV transmissions and plays).

Windermere, Cumbria. Windermere 3748.

MacDiarmid, Hugh (C. M. Grieve)
Born Langholm 1892. Educ. Langholm Academy; Broughton School, Edinburgh. Hon. LLD, Edinburgh. Planned to be a teacher but took up journalism. As the pioneer of the Scottish literary renaissance in the '20s and by his poetry, mainly in the Scots language he revitalised, he has been a powerful influence on modern Scottish writing as well as achieving an international reputation as one of the great poets of his time. His output has been enormous and includes the following:

Poetry: Sangshaw (1925, Blackwood). Penny Wheep (1926, Blackwood). A Drunk Man Looks at the Thistle (1926, Blackwood). To Circumjack Cencrastus (1930, Blackwood). First Hymn to Lenin (1931, Unicorn). Stony Limits (1932, Gollancz). Scots Unbound (1932, Mackay, Stirling). Second Hymn to Lenin (1935, Nott). A Kist of Whistles (1947, Maclellan). Three Hymns to Lenin (1957, Castle Wynd). Selected Poems (1955, Maclellan). Collected Poems (1962, Oliver & Boyd). More Collected Poems (1970, MacGibbon & Kee). Selected Poems (1970, Penguin).

Prose: Annals of the Five Senses (1923). Contemporary Scottish Studies (1926, re-issued 1976, *Scottish Educational Journal*). Albyn, or the Future of Scotland (1927, Kegan Paul). The Scottish Scene, with Lewis Grassic Gibbon (1934, Jarrold). At the Sign of the Thistle (1934, Nott). Scottish Eccentrics (1936, Routledge). The Islands of Scotland (1939, Batsford). Lucky Poet (1943, Methuen). The Company I've Kept (1966, Hutchinson). The Uncanny Scot (1968, MacGibbon & Kee). Selected Essays (1969, Cape). John Knox, in New Assessments (1976, Ramsay Head).

MacDonald, Donald John
Born South Uist 1919.

Sguaban Eorna (1974, Club Leabhar). Fo Sgail a' Swastica (1974, Club Leabhar).

2 Peninerine, Lochboisdale, South Uist.

Macdonald, Norman Malcolm
Born Thunder Bay, Canada, 1927. Educ. Newbattle Abbey Coll. Born Canada of Lewis parents, brought up in Lewis, National Service in RAF overseas, eight years in New Zealand Air Force, eight years in London. Worked as clerk, labourer, journalist, has own croft.

Creach Mhor Nam Fiadh (1973, *Stornoway Gazette*). The Catechist, the Bard and Their Women (1974, French). An Ceistear, am Bard 's na Boirionnaich (1974, Club Leabhar). Calum Tod—Thirteen linked stories (1976, Club Leabhar). Call na H-Iolaire (Club Leabhar, 1976).

Screenplay: The Storm Witch. The Iolaire Disaster, dramatised documentary, BBC Radio 1969. Five Gaelic Plays, BBC Radio 1970. Torquil's Seed (1976, Stornoway). Seonaidh, Bathach Chaluim (1970, 1975, Stornoway). An Ceistear, am Bard 's na Boirionnaich (1974, Montrose).

14 Tong, Isle of Lewis. Stornoway 2965.

Macdougall, Carl
Born Glasgow 1941. Senior Secondary. Has had poetry and prose published in a number of Scottish magazines and has broadcast frequently. Worked extensively on creative writing projects through Scottish Arts Council Writers in School scheme. Written many folksongs; best known is probably *Cod Liver Oil and Orange Juice.* Joint Editor *Chapbook.*

A Cuckoo's Nest (1974, Molendinar). Ascent of Water (1975, Molendinar). Scottish Short Stories (1976, Collins).

50 Craigievar Drive, Pitteuchar, Glenrothes, Fife FY4 4AN. Glenrothes 773472.

McDuff, David
Born Sale, Cheshire, 1945. Educ. George Watson's Coll., Edinburgh; Univ. of Edinburgh. Has lived for spells in Cambridge, England; Moscow, USSR; Tuscany, Italy; York, England; Boston, Massachussetts.

Words in Nature (1971, Ramsay Head Press). Osip Mandel'shtam, Selected Poems (1973, Rivers Press, Cambridge). Osip Mandelstam, Selected Poems (revised edition) (1975, Farrar, Straus & Giroux, New York).

Tjarnargata 41, Reykjavik, Iceland.

McGeoch, Andrew Jackson
Born Glasgow 1900. Educ. Kelvinside Academy, Larchfield School, Mill Hill. Entered family firm of marine equipment manufacturers, 1919. Spent several years in London office. Married 1940, one daughter. Army 1939-41. Retired from business in 1962 to devote more time to writing.

Annus Mirabilis: Poems (1949, Heinemann). The Alighting Leaf: Poems (1960, Putnam). The Golden Calf: Play, under name Adrian Paul (1966, Canopy Press). Themes and Variations: Poems (1969, privately).

6 Carruth Drive, Kilmacolm, Renfrewshire PA13 4HR. Kilmacolm 3279.

McGrath, John
Founder of the 7:84 Theatre Company, which tours throughout Scotland. Former BBC Television producer. Creator of Z Cars, for which he wrote the early scripts.

Plays: Events While Guarding a Bofors Gun (filmed). The Cheviot, the Stag and the Black, Black Oil (1974, West Highland Pub. Co.). The Game's a Bogey. Boom. My Pal and Me. The Little Red Hen. Honour Your Partner.

McGrath, Tom
Born 1940. Director of Third Eye, Scottish Arts Council Glasgow art centre. Poet, editor, jazz musician, founder editor of *International Times.*

The Buddha Poems (Midnight Press).

350 Sauchiehall Street, Glasgow G2 3JD.

McIlvanney, William
Born Kilmarnock 1936. Educ. Kilmarnock Academy, Glasgow Univ. Married, two children. Teaching since 1960, with two breaks: 1970-71—teaching Eng. Lit. and Creative writing to American students doing foreign year at Univ. of Grenoble; 1972-73 — Creative Writing Fellow at Univ. of Strathclyde. In 1975, resigned post as Assistant Rector (Curriculum) at Greenwood Academy (Irvine)—currently teaching as Assistant for two days per week, writing rest of time.

Remedy is None: Novel (1966, Eyre & Spottiswoode—Joint winner of Geoffrey Faber Memorial Award, 1967). A Gift from Nessus: Novel (1968, Eyre Methuen—Scottish

Arts Council Publication Award, 1969). The Longships in Harbour: Poems (1970, Eyre Methuen). Docherty: Novel (1975, Allen & Unwin—Whitbread Award for Fiction, 1975).
Play: The Attic (Premier August, 1975, Irvine; subsequently performed at Ochtertyre and Edinburgh Festival Fringe).
25 Ellis Street, Kilmarnock. Kilmarnock 21063.

McIntyre, Lorn
Work includes poetry and short stories. Made a study of the poetry of Iain Crichton Smith at Stirling Univ.
Blood on the Moon (1974, Club Leabhar).

Mackay, James Alexander
Born Inverness 1936. Educ. Hillhead High School, Glasgow; Glasgow Univ. Short Service commission in the Army; served in the Outer Hebrides (Guided Weapons Range, 1959-61). Assistant Keeper, British Museum, London 1971-71, Department of Printed Books. Freelance writer since 1959. Returned to Scotland in 1972 as a full-time writer.
St Kilda: Its Posts and Communications (1963, Scottish Postmark Group). The Tapling Collection (1964, British Museum). World of Stamps (1964, Johnson). Tristan da Cunha: Its Postal History and Philately (1965, Crabb, Ewell). Commonwealth Stamp Design, 1840-1965 (1965, British Museum). Churchill on Stamps (1966, privately published). The Story of Malta and her Stamps (1966, Collecta). The Story of Great Britain and her Stamps (1967, Collecta). Make Money with Stamps (1966, Collecta). Learn About Stamps (1967, Collecta). Cover Collecting (1967, Collecta). Money in Stamps (1967, Johnson Publications). Value in Coins and Medals (1968, Johnson Publications). The Story of Eire and her Stamps (1969, Collecta). The Story of East Africa and its Stamps (1970, Collecta). Antiques of the Future (1970, Studio Vista; 1971, Universe Books, New York). An Introduction to Small Antiques (1970, Garnstone Press). Commemorative Medals (1970, Arthur Barker). Commemorative Pottery and Porcelain (1971, Garnstone Press). Coin-collecting for Grown-up Beginners (1971, Garnstone Press). Airmails 1870-1970 (1971, Batsford). Greek and Roman Coins 1971, Barker). Undiscovered Antiques (1971, Garnstone Press). The World of Classic Stamps (Putnam, New York). Glass Paperweights (1973, Ward Lock). Animalier Bronzes (1973, Ward Lock). Dictionary of Stamps of the World (1973, Michael Joseph). Source Book of Stamps (1974, Ward Lock). A History of Stamp Design (1974, Peter Lowe). Turn of the Century Antiques (1974, Ward Lock). Robert Bruce, King of Scots (1974, Hale). The Encyclopaedia of Small Antiques (1975, Ward Lock). The Price Guide to Collectable Antiques (1975, Antique Collector's Club). Rural Crafts in Scotland (1976, Hale).
Under nom-de-plume of Ian Angus (all Ward Lock publications): Collecting Antiques 1972). Stamps, Posts and Postmarks (1973). Coins and Money Tokens (1973). Medals and Decorations (1973). Paper Money (1974).
Translations: (from French)—Postal History by Prince Dmitri Kandaouroff (1973, Peter Lowe). (From Dutch)—The New World Encyclopaedia, 3 vols. (1974, Ward Lock).
Editor-in-Chief, IPC *World Stamp Encyclopedia* (weekly partwork, 1969-72). *Financial Times* columnist on antique-collection (1967-71), numismatics and philately (1972-   ).
11 Newall Terrace, Dumfries DG1 1LN. 0387-5250.

Mackenzie, Robert Fraser
Born Lethenty, Aberdeenshire, 1910. Educ. Turriff School; Gordon's College, Aberdeen; University of Aberdeen. Travelled widely in Europe (by bicycle). Africa and USA. Navigator, RAF. Headmaster, Braehead School, Fife; and Summerhill Academy, Aberdeen.
Road Fortune, with Hunter Diack (1935, Macmillan). A Question of Living (1963, Collins). Escape from the Classroom (1965, Collins). The Sins of the Children (1967, Collins). State School (1970, Penguin).

Programmes for Schools (radio and television); *Times Ed. Supplement* articles on education.

West Cults Farm, Cults, Aberdeenshire. Aberdeen 47780.

Mackie, Albert David
Born Edinburgh 1904. Educ. Broughton School, Edinburgh Univ. Has been a journalist in Jamaica, Glasgow, Edinburgh. Editor, Edinburgh *Evening Dispatch*, 1946-54. Married, one son, two daughters. Widely known for his humorous topical verses under the name "Macnib."

Poems in Two Tongues (1928, Darien Press). Sing a Sang o Scotland (1944, Maclellan). A Call from Warsaw (1944, Polish Library). The Hearts (1958, Stanley Paul). The Book of MacNib (1960, Castle Wynd). Scottish Pageantry (1967, Hutchinson). Donald's Dive (1971, Macdonald). The Scotch Comedians (1973, Ramsay Head Press). Scotch Whisky Drinker's Companion (1973, Ramsay Head Press). *Plays:* The Hogmanay Story, Festival City, Hame, Sheena, MacHattie's Hotel (all at Gateway Theatre, Edinburgh).

27 Blackford Avenue, Edinburgh EH9 2PJ. 031-667 3227.

Mackie, Alastair W.
Born Aberdeen 1925. Skene Square School, Robert Gordon's College, Aberdeen Univ. Soundings (1966, Akros). Clytach (1972, Akros). A Hielant Sequence (1974, Akros).

13 St Adrian's Place, Anstruther. Anstruther 310775.

Mackintosh, John P.
Born 1929. Educ. Melville Coll., Edinburgh; Edinburgh Univ.; Balliol Coll., Oxford; Princeton Univ., New Jersey. Married, two sons, two daughters. D.Litt., Edinburgh Univ., 1967. Senior Lecturer in Government Univ., Ibadan, 1961-63. Professor of Politics, Strathclyde Univ., 1965-66. Visiting Professor of Government, Birkbeck Coll., London Univ., since 1972. Elected Labour MP for Berwick and East Lothian in 1966 and again in 1974. Governor, Atlantic Inst. for International Affairs, Paris, 1970. Member, Chatham House Research Comm., 1973. Fellow, Royal Historical Soc., 1973. Chairman, Hansard Soc., 1974. Chairman, Scot. Labour Comm. for Europe, 1975. Joint editor, *Political Quarterly*, July 1975.

The British Cabinet (1962, Stevens). Nigerian Politics and Government (1966, Allen & Unwin). The Devolution of Power (1968, Hodder). The Government and Politics of Britain (1970, Hutchinson).

McKillop, Menzies
Born 1929. Educ. Glasgow Univ. Taught in Glasgow schools until 1975. Winner of BBC Science Fiction Short Story Competition, 1971.

Parkland Poets No. 3 (1969, Akros). Poems in Scottish Poetry 2, 3, 4 and 5 (Edin. Univ. Press) and Scottish Love Poems (Canongate).

Play: The Future Pit (1976, Guthrie 2 Theatre, Minneapolis, USA). This play is also published in Guthrie New Theatre Vol. 1 (Grove Press, New York). Many radio plays for BBC and Canadian Broadcasting Corporation. Also short stories on BBC Radio 4.

8 Fergus Court, Glasgow G20 6AR. 041-946 6913.

MacKinnon, Kenneth
Born London 1933. Educ. London Univ. B.Sc.(Econ.) 1954, M.A.(Educ.) 1971, Ph.D. 1975. Teacher, Lecturer. Member: Liberal Party, Methodist Church, British Sociological Association, An Comunn Gaidhealach. Mayor, Southend-on-Sea 1965-66. (Council member 1958-70, Chairman Town Planning 1962-65, 66-67).

The Lion's Tongue (1974, Club Leabhar). Language, Education and Social Processes in a Gaelic Community (1976, Routledge).

Broadcast talks on Gaelic sociolinguistics on Gaelic services of CBC, BBC. Frequent contributor to popular and academic press on sociolinguistics, education and social problems of the Gaidhealtachd.

Hatfield Polytechnic, School of Social Sciences. 0702-525402; 07072-68100, Ext. 439.

Maclean, Alister
Born 1922. Educ. Glasgow Univ. Was a schoolteacher in Scotland before becoming a novelist. Now lives abroad.

Ulysses (1955). The Guns of Navarone (1957). South by Java Head (1959). Last Frontier (1960). Night Without End (1960). Fear is the Key (1961). Golden Rendezvous (1962). All About Lawrence of Arabia (1962). Ice Station Zebra (1963). When Eight Bells Toll (1966). Where Eagles Dare (1967). Force Ten from Navarone (1968). Puppet on a Chain (1969). Bear Island (1971). Captain Cook (1972). *As Ian Stuart:* Dark Crusader (1961). Snow on the Ben (1961). The Satan Bug (1962). All Collins. The Way to Dusty Death (1973). Breakheart Pass (1974). The Golden Gate (1976).

Maclean, Campbell
Educ. Glasgow Univ. Minister of Cramond Parish Church, Edinburgh; formerly at Campbeltown. Past editor of *Contact* and literary editor of *New Scotland*. Warwick Lecturer to Scottish Univs., 1974-76. BBC Television interviewer and presenter.

John Knox, with Hugh MacDiarmid and Anthony Ross (1976, Ramsay Head Press).

Maclean, Allan Campbell
Born Barrow-in-Furness 1922. Educ. Elementary. Started working life as apprentice motor mechanic. After war service with RAF in Western Desert, Tripolitania, Tunisia, Sicily, Italy and Austria, bought secondhand typewriter and started career as writer, thoughtfully using several pseudonyms. Fourteen novels and one work of non-fiction published under own name. Contested Inverness-shire as Labour candidate in 1964 and 1966. Former Chairman, Scottish Council of the Labour Party.

The Hill of the Red Fox (1955, Collins). Storm Over Skye (1956, Collins). Master of Morgana (1960, Collins). Ribbon of Fire (1962, Collins). The Islander (1962, Collins). A Sound of Trumpets (1967, Collins). The Glasshouse (1969, Calder & Boyars). The Year of the Stranger (1971, Collins). The Highlands & Islands of Scotland (1976, Collins).

Scripted films: Highlands. A Pride of Islands. Two Men of Tiree.

Anerley Cottage, 16 Kingsmills Road, Inverness. 0463-34815.F

Maclean, Sir Fitzroy
Born 1911. Educ. Eton, Cambridge. Resigned from Diplomatic Service in 1939, joined Cameron Highlanders, later SAS. Commanded British mission to Jugoslav partisans. Under-Sec. of State for War, 1954-57.

Eastern Approaches (1949). Disputed Barricade (1957). A Person for England (1958). Back to Bokhara (1959). Jugoslavia (1969). Concise History of Scotland (1970). Battle of Neretva (1970). To Caucasus (1976).

Maclean, Sorley
Born 1911.

17 Poems for 6d, with Robert Garioch (1940). Dain do Eimhir (1943). Four points of a Saltire, with others (1970, Reprographia). Poems to Eimhir, trans. from the Gaelic by Iain Crichton Smith (1971, Gollancz).

McLellan, Robert
Born Lanark 1907. Educ. Bearsden Academy, Goasgow Univ. Married, one son, one daughter. War service, Royal Artillery 1940-46. Member of Arran District Council, 1956-65. Chairman Scottish Sub-Comm. League of Dramatists 1952-61. Chairman Scottish Sub-Comm. Society of Authors 1961-65. Pres. District Councils Assoc. for Scotland 1962-64. Hon. Vice-Pres. Lallans Society 1972- . Hon. Pres. Scottish Society of Playwrights 1975- .

Plays, in Scots: Jeddart Justice (1934, Bone and Hulley). The Changeling—in Scottish One-Act Plays (1938, Porpoise Press). Toom Byres (1947, Maclellan). The Carlin Moth, in verse in North Light (1947, Maclellan). The Cailleach (1948, Donaldson). Torwatletie (1950, Maclellan). The Hypocrite (1970, Calder & Boyars). Jamie the Saxt (1971, Calder & Boyars).

Topographical and historical, in English: The Isle of Arran (1969, David and Charles).
Play productions: Jeddart Justice (1933, Curtain Theatre, Glasgow). Tarfessock (1934, Curtain Theatre, Glasgow). The Changeling (1934, Dumbarton People's Theatre). Cian and Ethne (1935, Curtain Theatre, Glasgow). Toom Byres (1936, Curtain Theatre Company in Lyric Theatre, Glasgow). Jamie the Saxt (1937, Curtain Theatre Company in Lyric Theatre). Portrait of an Artist (1939, Curtain Theatre Company in Lyric Theatre). Torwatletie (1946, Glasgow Unity Theatre Company in Queen's Theatre, Glasgow). The Carlin Moth (1947, SCDA Festival, Lyric Theatre, Glasgow). The Flouers o Edinburgh (1948, Glasgow Unity Theatre Company in King's Theatre, Edinburgh; Edinburgh Festival production 1958 by Gateway Company). The Cailleach (1948, Arran SCDA Festival). The Smuggler (1949, Arran SCDA Festival). Mary Stewart (1951, Glasgow Citizens' Theatre). The Road to the Isles (1954, Glasgow Citizens' Theatre). Young Auchinleck (1962, Gateway Theatre; an Edinburgh Festival production). The Hypocrite (1967, Edinburgh Lyceum Theatre).
Television: Plays: Rab Mossgeil (1960). Young Auchinleck (1963). Verse: Island Burn, in the series Poets' Places (1965).
Radio: Plays: The Carlin Moth (1946). As Ithers See Us (1954). Rab Mossgiel (1959). Balloon Tytler (1962). The Old Byre at Clashmore (1965). Verse: Sweet Largie Bay (1956; Poetry Prize, Scottish Committee of the Arts Council 1955-56). Short Stories: Linmill, four series, of six stories each, broadcast between 1960 and 1965.
High Corrie, Isle of Arran KA27 8TB. 077 081 289.

MacLeod, Ellen Jane (Mrs)
Born Glasgow 1918. Educ. in Glasgow and American schools. Worked seven years as an executive assistant to Head Librarian at Fort Vancouver Regional Library. There is an Ellen Jane MacLeod Collection at the University of Southern Mississippi and in the Washington Authors Collection at Washington State Library.
The Seven Wise Owls (1956, Pickering & Inglis). Alaska Star (1957, Pickering & Inglis). Adventures on Lazy "N" (1957, Pickering & Inglis). Crooked Signpost (Ella Anderson pseud.) (1957, Pickering & Inglis). Fourth Window (1957, Cowman Pub. USA). Hawaiian Lei (Ella Anderson pseud.) (1958, Pickering & Inglis). Jo-Jo (Ella Anderson pseud.) (1959, Pickering & Inglis). Mystery Gorge (1959, Pickering & Inglis). Mystery of Tolling Bell (1960, Pickering & Inglis). Vanishing Light (Ella Anderson pseud.) (1960, Pickering & Inglis). Talking Mountain (1961, Pickering & Inglis). Orchids for a Rose (1963, Arcadia House, USA). Island in the Mist (1965, Bethany Press, USA). Stranger in the Glen (1968, Arcadia House, USA). Broken Melody (1969, Arcadia House USA). Trouble at Circle "G" (1969, Pickering & Inglis). The Kelpie Ledge (1973, Lenox Hill Press USA). Isle of Shadows (1974, Lenox Hill Press USA).
Radio plays: One Stormy Night (1964, BBC). Something Fishy (1966, BBC).
12 Montgomery Place, Buchlyrie, Stirlingshire FK8 3NF.

Macleod, Joseph Todd Gorden
Born Ealing, Middlesex, 1903. Educ. Rugby; Balliol Coll., Oxford; Inner Temple. Married (1) Kit Macgregor Davis, Uddingston; (2) Maria Teresa Foscina, Rome; one son, one daughter. Has been reviewer, actor, play director, lecturer on theatre since 1955. Director, Festival Theatre, Cambridge, 1933-36. BBC Announcer, 1938-45. Managing Director, Scottish National Film Studios, 1946-47.
Beauty and the Beast (1927, Chatto). The Ecliptic Poem (1930, Faber). Foray of Centaurs: poem (1931, This Quarter, Paris). Overture to Cambridge: novel (1936, Allen & Unwin). New Soviet Theatre (1943, Allen & Unwin). Actors Cross the Volga (1946, Allen & Unwin). A Job at the BBC (1947, Maclellan). Soviet Theatre Sketchbook (1951, Allen & Unwin). The Passage of the Torch: poem (1951, Oliver & Boyd). Short History of the British Theatre (1958, Sansoni, Florence). People of Florence (1968, Allen & Unwin). The Sisters D'Aranyi (1969, Allen & Unwin). An Old Olive Tree: poems (1971, Macdonald, Scot. Arts Council Award). *Plays:* The Suppliants of Aeschylus (1932, Cambridge). A Woman Turned to Stone (1934, Cambridge). Overture to Cambridge (1934, Cambridge). A Miracle for St George (1935, Cambridge). Leap in September (1952, Perth, Arts Council Award).

106

Under pseud. Adam Drinan: The Cove (1940, privately) Men of the Rocks (1942, Fortune). Ghosts of the Strath (1943, Fortune). Women of the Happy Island (1944, Maclellan). Script from Norway (1953, Maclellan).
Via Delle Ballodole 9/7, Trespiano 50139, Firenze, Italy. Firenze 417056.

Macleod, Sheila
The Moving Accident (1967). The Snow White Soliloquies (1970). Letters from the Portuguese (1971).

MacMillan, Hector
Born and brought up in the east end of Glasgow. Worked abroad for ten years but chose to return to Scotland because he wanted to be involved in the exciting changes that were taking place.
The Sash My Father Wore (1974, Molendinar). First performance at Edinburgh Festival Fringe, 1973; Pavilion Theatre, Glasgow, 1974.

Macmillan, James
National newspaper leader writer, specialising in industrial and economic affairs.
The American Take-over of Britain (Frewin). The Honours Game (Frewin). Anatomy of Scotland (1969, Frewin).

McMillan, Roddy
Play: The Bevellers (1974, Southside).

Macnab, Peter Angus
Born Portmahomack, Ross-shire. Retired banker. Former Ayrshire County Councillor.
The Isle of Mull (1970, David & Charles). Many articles of Scottish topography and folklore.
Fairway, Seamill, West Kilbride, Ayrshire KA23 9HP. West Kilbride 823291.

MacNeill, Duncan Harald
Born Orkney 1892. Educ. Kirkwall Academy, Glasgow Univ., Edinburgh Univ. Served 1914-19 with 52nd Division and Indian Army. Settled in Inverness in 1921. Married, three sons. Founder member Highland Rugby Club. Vice-chairman National Party of Scotland, 1932-   . FSA Scot.
The Scottish Realm (1947, A. & J. Donaldson). Art and Science of Government among the Scots (1958, Maclellan). Historical Scottish Constitution (1973, Albyn Press).
9 Ardross Street, Inverness. Inverness 32081.

McNeil, Neil
Born Greenock 1940. Educ. Greenock High; Ruskin Coll., Oxford. Former draughtsman. Has worked in New Towns, Livingston and Milton Keynes, on community development. Urban environment project in Glasgow. Founder member Inter. Poetry Soc., member Glasgow Ballad Club, Lallans Soc., Saltire Soc. Co-founder Rannoch Gillamoor Poets. Designs formats on printed material for community work and poetry volumes. Co-editor of poetry quarterly *Strath.*
Timescales, poems in Scots and English (1975, Hippopotamus Press). Poems in various anthologies and journals.
76 Hawthorn Road, Abronhill, Cumbernauld, Glasgow G67 3LY.

Macnicol, Eona (Kathleen)
Born Inverness 1910. Educ. Inverness Royal Academy, Edinburgh Univ. Lived for some years in India, where husband taught in college. Active in World Development Movement and Amnesty International.
Colum of Derry: Novel (1955, Sheed & Ward). Lamp in the Night Wind: Novel (1964, Maclellan). The Hallowe'en Hero: Short stories (1969, Blackwood).
The Manse, Newtongrange, Midlothian. 031-663 2140.

Macpherson, Margaret
Born Colinton, Midlothian, 1908. Educ. private school, Edinburgh Univ. Married
1929. Lived in Skye ever since. Member HIDB Consultative Council. Sec. local Labour
Party.
The Shinty Boys (1963, Collins). The Rough Road (1965, Collins). Ponies for Hire
(1967, Collins). The New Tenants (1968, Collins). The Battle of the Braes (1972,
Collins). The Boy on the Roof (1974, Collins).
Ardrannach, Torvaig, Portree, Skye.

MacVicar, Angus
Born 1908, son of the manse. Educ. Glasgow Univ. Has lived most of his life on the
Mull of Kintyre. Has written over 65 books and hundreds of scripts for the BBC.
His most successful book, Salt in My Porridge: Confessions of a Minister's Son, now
in paperback, was published in 1971 (Hutchinson).

McWilliam, Colin E.
Born London 1928. Educ. Charterhouse; Caius Coll., Cambridge. Officer i/c Scottish
National Buildings Rocord 1953-57. Asst. Sec. National Trust for Scotland 1957-64.
Senior lecturer Edinburgh College of Art, Heriot-Watt Univ. 1964- . General Editor,
Buildings of Scotland (Penguin Books). Chairman, Scottish Georgian Society.
Scottish Townscape (Collins, 1975).
27 Warriston Crescent, Edinburgh EH3 5LB.

Mair, Alastair
Born Mauchline 1924. M.B., Ch.B. Pres. Scottish PEN, 1956-70. Shared Frederick
Niven Award, 1962. Novels include The Douglas Affair (1966, Heinemann) and The
Ripening Time (1970, Heinemann).

Mair, George Brown
Born Troon 1914. Educ. Mauchline village school; Kilmarnock Acad.; Glasgow Univ.
Married, two sons. M.B., Ch.B., M.D., F.R.C.S. Edinburgh and Glasgow. Fellow,
Royal Scottish Geographical Soc. Member, Scottish PEN, Soc. of Authors, Crime
Writers' Assoc., Guild of Travel Writers, Mystery Writers of America.
Surgery of Abdominal Hernia (1948, Arnold). Surgeon's Saga (1949, Heinemann).
Doctor Goes East (1957, Owen). Doctor Goes North (1958, Owen). Doctor Goes
West (1958, Owen). Doctor in Turkey (1961, Hale). Doctor in Moscow (1960, Jenkins).
The Day Kruschev Panicked (1961, Cassell). Death's Foot Forward (1963, Jarrold).
Miss Turquoise (1964, Jarrold). Live Love and Cry (1965, Jarrold). Kisses from
Satan (1966, Jarrold). Girl from Peking (1967, Jarrold). Black Champagne (1968,
Jarrold). Goddesses Never Die (1969, Jarrold). A Wreath of Amaelias (1970, Jarrold).
Crimson Jade (1971, Jarrold). Paradise Spells Danger (1973, Jarrold). Confessions of a
Surgeon (1974, Luscombe). Escape from Surgery (1975, Luscombe). World lecture
tours, frequently on TV and radio, writes a weekly medical column and monthly travel
page.
Upper Kinneil House, Old Polmont, Stirlingshire. 0324-62723.

Marshall, Bruce
Born Edinburgh. Educ. Edinburgh Academy; Glenalmond; St Andrews Univ; Edin-
burgh Univ. Lost right leg in World War One. Worked as chartered accountant in
Paris, 1926-40. Royal Pay Corps, Intelligence and Allied Commission for Austria,
1940-46.
Father Malachy's Miracle (1931, Heinemann). Yellow Tapers for Paris (1943, Constable). George Brown's Schooldays (1945, Constable). The Red Danube (1947,
Constable). Every Man a Penny (1949, Constable). The White Rabbit (1952, Evans).
The Fair Bride (1952, Constable). The Bishop (1970, Constable). Urban the Ninth
(1972, Constable).
104 Boulevard du Cap, Antibes, France.

Mavor, Ronald
Born 1925. Educ. Merchiston Castle School, Edinburgh; Glasgow Univ. Practised medicine until 1957. Drama critic, *The Scotsman*, 1957-65. Director, Scottish Arts Council, 1965-71. Vice chairman, Edinburgh Festival Council.

Books: Art the Hard Way (1972). A Private Matter (1974). *Plays:* The Keys of Paradise (1959). Aurelia (1960). Muir of Huntershill (1962). The Partridge Dance (1963). A Private Matter (1973). The Quartet (1974). The Doctors.

Miller, Karl
Born and educ. in Edinburgh. Has been literary editor of the *Spectator* and *New Statesman* and editor of *The Listener*.

Edit. Memoirs of a Modern Scotland (1970). Cockburn's Millennium (1976, Duckworth).

Millington, Rosemary Irene
Born Glasgow 1935. Educ. Convent of Sacred Heart, Hove; Brighton Art School; Alliance Francaise, Paris. Trained as artist. Did two years as student nurse at Middlesex Hospital. Joined BBC in 1957. Went to Australia 1959, worked mainly in Outback. Returned to BBC and Scotland 1961. Left BBC 1971.

A Nation of Trees (1962, New Authors). The Islanders (1965, Hutchinson).

Hillhead, Corse, Lumphanan, Aberdeenshire, AB3 4RD. Lumphanan 625.

Mitchison, Naomi
Born Edinburgh 1897. Born Haldane, married Dick Mitchison (later Lord Mitchison of Carradale, Labour peer). Five children, nineteen grandchildren. Stood as Labour candidate for Scottish Universities, member Highland Advisory Panel, Highland Consultative Council, etc. Argyll County Council, presently chairman East Kintyre Community Council. Member of Bakgatla of Botswana.

Some seventy books including The Corn King and the Spring Queen (1931, Cape). The Blood of the Martyrs (1939, Constable). The Bull Calves (1945, Cape). To the Chapel Perilous (1954, Allen & Unwin). Diary of a Space Woman (1960, Gollancz). When We Become Men (1964, Collins). Cleopatra's People (1971, Heinemann). Small Talk (1974, Bodley Head). All Change Here (1975). Also many children's books.

Carradale, Campbeltown, Argyll. Carradale 234.

Moncrieffe of that Ilk, Sir Iain
11th Bt. Born 1919. Educ. Stowe, Heidelbirg, Oxford, Edinburgh. Capt. Scots Guards, 1939-46.

Simple Heraldry, with D. Pottinger (1953). Simple Custom (1954). Blood Royal (1956). The Highland Clans, with David Hicks (1967).

Montgomerie, William
Born Glasgow 1904. Educ. M.A. Glasgow, Ph.D. Edinburgh. With his wife Norah made several collections of Scottish folk rhymes and tales. Made detailed study of the MSS sources of the Scottish ballads and folk songs. Has lived for long periods in Berlin, Provence and Andalucia. Chairman, Assoc. for Liberal Studies.

Via: Poems (1933, Boriswood-Bodley Head). Squared Circle: Long poem (1934, Boriswood-Bodley Head). Scottish Nursery Rhymes, with Norah Montgomerie (1946, Hogarth). New Judgements, Robert Burns (1947, Maclellan). Sandy Candy, with N.M. (1948, Hogarth). Well at the World's End, Scottish Folktales, with N.M. (1956, Hogarth). Hogarth Book of Scottish Nursery Rhymes, with N.M. (1964, Hogarth). A Book of Scottish Nursery Rhymes, with N.M. (1965, OUP, New York). Three Poems (Duncan of Jordanstone Coll. of Art, n.d.). Poetry in various anthologies. Poems and short stories on radio.

131 Warrender Park Road, Edinburgh. 031-229 3843.

Morgan, Edwin
Born Glasgow 1920. Educ. Rutherglen Academy; High School of Glasgow; Glasgow Univ. At present titular professor of English, Glasgow Univ.

The Vision of Cathkin Braes (1952, Maclellan). Beowulf (1952, Hand & Flower Press). The Cape of Good Hope (1955, Peter Russell). Poems from Eugenio Montale (1959, Univ. of Reading School of Art). Sovpoems (1961, Migrant Press). Starryveldt (1965, Gomringer Press, Switzerland). Scotch Mist (1965, Renegade Press, Cleveland). Emergent Poems (1967, Hansjorg Mayer, Stuttgart). The Second Life (1968, Edin. Univ. Press). Gnomes (1968, Akros). Proverbfolder (1969, Openings Press). Penguin Modern Poets 15, with Alan Bold and Edward Brathwaite (1969, Penguin). Twelve Songs (1970, Castlelaw Press). The Horseman's Word (1970, Akros). Wi the Haill Voice (1972, Carcanet Press). Glasgow Sonnets (1972, Castlelaw Press). Instamatic Poems (1972, Ian McKelvie). The Whittrick (1973, Akros). From Glasgow to Saturn (1973, Carcanet Press). Essays (1974, Carcanet Press). Fifty Renascence Love-Poems (1975, Whiteknights Press).

Visual poems in many international exhibitions; opera librettos.

19 Whittingehame Court, Glasgow G12 0BG. 041-339 6260.

Morrice, Ken
Born Aberdeen 1924. Educ. Robert Gordon's Coll.; Aberdeen Univ. Brought up in Aberdeen. Qualified in Medicine. Served RNVR. Later specialised in psychiatry. Lived for some years in Scottish Borders, USA and Lancashire. Married: 1 son 2 daughters.

Prototype (1965, Macdonald). Crisis Intervention (1976, Pergamon Press).
In various anthologies.

30 Carnegie Crescent, Aberdeen.

Morrison, David
Born Glasgow 1941. Educ. Glasgow High School; Hamilton Academy; Strathclyde Univ. Lived in Glasgow, rural Lanarkshire, East Kilbride, Livingston, Caithness (present). Editor, *Scotia Review*. Associate of Library Association. Divisional Librarian for Caithness/Sutherland. Secretary, Scamp. Chairman, Wick Folk Club.

The Saxon Toon an Ither Poems (1966, Macdonald). The White Hind and Other Poems (1968, Caithness Books). The Clay Yard (1970, Scotia). The Winter Aisling (1971, Scotia). Edit. Essays on Neil M. Gunn (1971, Caithness Books). White Witch, White Woman (1972, Scotia). Paddy's Market (1973, Scotia). Idealist and Other Stories (1974, Club Leabhar). Essays on Fionn MacColla (1974, Caithness Books). Hammer and Thistle, with Alan Bold (1975, Caithness Books).

3 Moray Street, Wick, Caithness. Wick 3703.

Morrison, N. (Nancy) Brysson
Born Scotland. Educ. Park School, Glasgow; Harvington College, London.

Breakers (1930, Murray). Solitaire (1932, Murray). The Gowk Storm (1933, Collins). When the Wind Blows (1937, Collins). The Strangers (1935, Collins). These Are My Friends: Verse (1946, Bles). The Winnowing Years (1950, Hogarth; won the first Frederick Niven Award). The Hidden Fairing (1951, Hogarth). The Keeper of Time (1933, Church of Scotland; 2nd edition, 1967, Christian Action). The Following Wind (1954, Hogarth). They Need No Candle (1957, Epworth Press). The Other Traveller (1957, Hogarth). Mary Queen of Scots (1960, Vista Books; won the Literary Guild Award, USA). Thea (1962, Hale). The Private Life of Henry VIII (1964, Hale). Hawort Harvest: The Lives of the Brontes (1969, Dent). King's Quiver: The Last Three Tudors (1972, Dent). True Minds: The Marriage of Thomas and Jane Carlyle (1974, Dent).

The Gowk Storm, The Hidden Fairing, The Other Traveller and Thea were all put on the radio as plays.

Caledonian Club, 32 Abercromby Place, Edinburgh.

Morrison, T. J.
Born Glasgow. Educ. Glasgow High School. Brother of March Cost and Nancy Brysson Morrison. On Glasgow *Evening News*, 1929-31. In Police Reserve, London, 1939-45. Founder member of Screenwriters' Assoc. Scenario editor, Associated British, Elstree, 1946-48.

The Truce Breaker (1929, Murray). Tony Potter (1930, Murray). The Cairn (1935, Collins). Queen of Spades (1936, Collins). It's Different Abroad (1936, Jarrold). Death Comes on Derby Day (1939, Jarrold). They're Home Again (1946, Jarrold). Numerous screenplays for Gaumont, Warner, Associated British.

244 Finchley Road, London NW3 6DJ. 01-435 7747.

Morton, Robert Scott
Born Edinburgh 1910. Educ. Merchiston Castle, Edinburgh Coll. of Art. Asst. Architect to Sir Edward Maufe, London. Asst. Architect to Sir Frank Mears, Edinburgh. Superintending Architect, Scottish Office (retired 1971). Asst. Architect Historic Buildings Council 1971- . War service with Royal Engineers 1942-45, Chindit Division, Burma. Council member Cockburn Assoc., Royal Incorp. of Architects in Scotland, Edinburgh Architectural Assoc. Hon. member, Saltire Society. Pres., Scot. Arts Club, 1956-58. Editor Edinburgh Architectural Assoc. Year Book, 1959-69.

The Architectural Profession, in the Edinburgh vol., Third Statistical Account of Scotland (1966, Collins). Farm Design section, Lothians vol., Buildings of Scotland (Penguin). Traditional Farm Architecture in Scotland (1975, Ramsay Head Press).

Muir, Augustus
Born Canada. Educ. George Heriot's School, Edinburgh; Edinburgh Univ. Lives in Essex.

Has written a large number of books including: The Third Warning, The Blue Bonnet, Scotland's Road of Romance, The Riddle of Garth, The Intimate Thoughts of John Baxter, Bookseller, Heather Track and High Road, Scottish Portrait.

Mulrine, Stephen
Born Glasgow 1937. Educ. Glasgow Univ. Married, two children. Lecturer in Liberal Studies at Glasgow School of Art 1969- . Extra-mural Lecturer in Creative writing at Glasgow Univ. 1969-74. Member of Board of Directors, Citizens' Theatre 1975- .

Four Glasgow University Poets (1969, Akros). Poems (1971, Akros).

BBC TV: The Chiel Amang Us, series (1974). Play, The Chicken Dinner (1974). BBC Radio 4, several plays. Radio Forth, series, Deacon Brodie (1975).

83 Fintry Drive, Glasgow. 041-649 2183.

Munro, Hugh
Born Glasgow 1909.

The Clydesiders (1961, Macdonald).

Munro, Robin
Born Island of Bute 1946. Educ. Douglas Ewart High School, Galloway; Aberdeen Univ.

Shetland, Like the World: Poems (1973, Triangle Press). The Land of the Mind: Poem (1975, Dent).

Craighlaw, Kirkcowan, Galloway.

Murray, Angus Wolfe
Novel: The End of Something Nice (1967).

Murray, John (Iain Moireach)
Born Barvas 1938. Educ. Nicolson Institute, Stornoway; Edinburgh Univ. Lived in Edinburgh, Glasgow and Lewis. Teacher in English, Musselburgh Grammar School 1961-69. Editorial Officer, Gaelic Books Council 1969-1975. Project Director, Bilingual Education Project 1975- .

An Aghaidh Choimheach (1973, Gairm Publications).

Numerous contributions (Gaelic) on radio.

Plays: Feumaidh Sinn a Bhith Gaireachdainn (1969, Glasgow Gaelic Drama Festival; Premier award). Balaich a' Chruidh (1970, Glasgow).

52 Lower Barvas, Isle of Lewis. Barvas 239.

Murray, W. H.
Member Countryside Commission for Scotland, 1968- . Chairman Scottish Countryside Activities Council, 1968- . President Scottish Mountaineering Club, 1962-64.

Mountaineering in Scotland (1947, Dent). Undiscovered Scotland (1951, Dent). Scottish Himalayan Expedition (1951, Dent). The Story of Everest (1953, Dent) Five Frontiers (1959, Dent). The Spurs of Troodos (1960, Dent). Maelstrom (1962, Secker & Warburg). Highland Landscape (1962, National Trust for Scotland). Dark Rose the Phoenix (1965, Secker & Warburg). The Hebrides (1966, Heinemann). Companion Guide to the West Highlands of Scotland (1968, Collins). The Real Mackay (1969, Heinemann). The Islands of Western Scotland (1973, Eyre Methuen). The Scottish Highlands (1976, Scottish Mountaineering Trust).

Lochwood, Loch Goil, Argyll. 030-13-226.

Nairne, Campbell
Born Perth 1910. Educ. Edinburgh Univ.; Paris Sorbonne; London Univ.

One Stair Up (1931, Porpoise Press).

Neill, William
Born Prestwick 1922. Educ. Prestwick High School, Ayr Grammar School, Ayr Academy, Edinburgh Univ. Served in Royal Air Force then worked a brief spell as copy-writer before becoming a mature student at Edinburgh. Took honours degree in Celtic Studies. Now earns living as teacher in Galloway.

Scotland's Castle (1969, Reprographia). Poems (1970, Akros). Four Points of a Saltire, with Maclean, Hay, MacGregor (1970, Reprographia). Despatches Home (1972, Reprographia). Buile Shuibhne (1974, Club Leabhar).

57 Main Street, Crossmichael, Castle Douglas. Crossmichael 265.

Niall, Ian
The Poacher's Handbook (1966). The Country Blacksmith (1968). The Fowler's World (1968). The Galloway Shepherd (1970). The Village Policeman (1971). The Forester (1972). A London Boyhood (1974, Heinemann).

Nicolson, Robert
Civil servant.

Mrs Ross (1961, Constable). A Flight of Steps (1966, Constable) as The Whisperers was filmed with Edith Evans and presented on radio and television.

Nimmo, Ian
Born India 1934. Educ. Royal School of Dunkeld, Breadalbane Academy. Commissioned in Royal Scots Fusiliers. Formerly editor of *Weekly Scotsman.* Appointed editor *Evening News* 1976.

Robert Burns, His Life and Traditions in Words and Sounds (1965, Record Books). Crossing the Tay (Hale). Portrait of Edinburgh (1969, Hale).

Nye, Robert
Born London 1939. Educ. Southend High School. Married, two daughters. Has lived in Edinburgh since 1967. Poetry editor, *The Scotsman,* 1967- . Poetry critic, *The Times,* 1971- . Writer in Residence, Edinburgh Univ., 1976-77. Member of vestry, St Michael and All Saints, Edinburgh.

Juvenalia 1—poems (1961, Scorpion Press). Juvenalia 2 (1963, Scorpion Press). Darker Ends—poems (1969, Calder & Boyars). Divisions on a Ground—poems

112

(1976, Carcanet Press). Doubtfire—novel (1967, Calder & Boyars). Tales I Told My Mother—stories (1969, Calder). Falstaff—novel (1976, Hamilton). *Edited:* A Choice of Sir Walter Raleigh's Verse (1972, Faber). William Barns of Dorset (1973, Carcanet). A Choice of Swinburne's Verse (1973, Faber). Faber Book of Sonnets (1976, Faber). The English Sermon 1750-1850 (1976, Carcanet). Beowulf—translation (1968, Faber). *Plays:* Sisters (1969, broadcast BBC; produced Edinburgh 1973). The Seven Deadly Sins—a masque (1974, St Mary's Cathedral, Edinburgh).

Oakley, Charles Allen
Born Portsmouth 1900. Educ. Devonport High School, Glasgow Univ. Apprenticeship John Brown's Shipyard, 1918-23. University lecturerships, Aberdeen Univ., Glasgow Univ., 1926-73. Scottish Controller, Ministry of Aircraft Production, 1939-45, and Board of Trade 1946-53. Chairman, Scottish Film Council, 1939-75. Has held office in innumerable organisations and directorships in various companies. Has had a lifelong interest in cinema and is an accomplished cartoonist. Editor, Glasgow Chamber of Commerce Journal, 1953- . Editor, Glasgow Corp. Annual Industrial Handbook, 1962-74.
Vocational Guidance (1935, Univ. of London Press). Scottish Industry Today (1937, Moray Press). Industrial Map of Scotland (1939, Oliver & Boyd). Men at Work (1945, Univ. of London Press). The Second City (1946, Blackie). Scottish Industry (1953, Collins). The Last Tram (1962, Glasgow Corp.). Where We Came In (1964, Allen & Unwin). History of a Faculty (1973, Glasgow Univ.). Dear Old Glasgow Town (1975, Blackie). Compiled Edwardian Newsreel, 1947, for British Film Institute, and various films from old Glasgow newsreels.
3a Cliveden Drive, Glasgow G12. 041-339 7000.

Oram, Neil
Born 1938.
Night Scene (1964, Lee Harwood). Children of Albion (1969, Penguin). Words Re-arranged (1973, Zum Zum). Past the Antique Pain (1974, Zum Zum). Beauty's Shit (1976, Zum Zum).
Grotaig, Durmnadrochit, Inverness-shire.

Paterson, Alexander Brown
Born St Andrews 1907. Journalist. Founder of the Byre Theatre, St Andrews and is chairman of its board. Former chairman, Fed. of Scottish Repertory Theatres and Go Theatre. Chairman, St Andrews Preservation Trust. Drama adjudicator and lecturer. MBE, Hon. MA St Andrews Univ.
All about Fife (annually, Fife Tourist Board). Portrait of Fife (1970, Outram). The Foreigner: Play (1969, St Andrews Times). Highland Games: Farce (1953, C. S. Russell, Anstruther).)
Plays: Re-union in St Andrews (1946, Byre Theatre, St Andrews). The Open (1949, Byre Theatre). The Herald's not for Sale (1952, Byre Theatre). Time is All (1955, Byre Theatre). Masque of the Cardinal (1965, Byre Theatre). The Lost Provost (1972, Byre Theatre), and many others.
White Gyle, Lade Braes, St Andrews. St Andrews 4493.

Paterson, Neil
Born Greenock 1916. Educ. Banff Academy, Edinburgh Univ. Lieut. RNVR in minesweepers, 1940-46. Atlantic Award in Literature, 1946. Award of American Academy of Motion Picture Arts and Sciences (Oscar), 1960. Director, Grampian TV. Member Arts Council of GB. Vice-chairman Scottish Arts Council. Member Films of Scotland. Governor, National Film School. Governor Pitlochry Festival Theatre. Former Governor, British Film Inst. Appointed Director, Films of Scotland, 1976.
The China Run (1948). Behold Thy Daughter (1950). And Delilah (1951). Man on the Tight Rope (1953). A Candle to the Devil (1972). Many film stories and screen plays.
St Ronans, Crieff, Perthshire. Crieff 2615.

H   113

Paulin, Dorothy Margaret
Born Dumfries 1904. M.A., B.Com., Edinburgh. Married 1931 Neil Godfrey Paulin, WS, one daughter. Editor *Gallovidian*, 1926-36. Poetry Section, *Poetry Review*, 1943-44, *Scottish Home and Country*, 1947-51. Liaison Officer, Dept. of Agric. for Scotland, 1942-47. Freelance writer. Farmer (retired). Scottish Representative, Soil Assoc. Council. Rep. on APRS Council. Chairman, Stewartry Preservation Soc.

Country Gold (1936). Wan Water (1939). Solway Tide (1951). Springtime by Loch Ken (1963).

Drumrash, Parton, Castle Douglas, DG7 3NF. Parton 274.

Perrie, Walter
Born village of Quarter, 1949. Educ. Hamilton Academy, Edinburgh Univ. Married. Founder and Editor *Chapman*. Chairman Scottish Assoc. of Magazine Publishers.

Deirdre (pseudonym P. MacCrimmon) (1971, Akros). Ulysses (1971, Russell-Calder Press). Plainsong (1974, Lothlorien). Poem on a Winter Night (1976, Macdonald).

118 Brankholm Brae, Hamilton, Lanarkshire.

Petzsch, Helmut
Born Berlin 1920. Educ. Hamburg; London; Coll. of Art, Edinburgh. Married, one son, two daughters. Teacher and artist. Society of Scottish Artists, 1952. Fellow, Soc. of Antiquaries of Scotland, 1965.

Architecture in Scotland (1971, Longman).

32 Canaan Lane, Edinburgh EH10 4SU. 031-447 2376.

Pilcher, Rosamunde
Born Lelant, Cornwall, 1924. Educ. St Clares, Penzance; Howell's School, Llandaff, S. Wales. Served in WRNS during the war, in Portsmouth, and then Trincomalee, Ceylon. Married 1946 Graham Pilcher, Director, Sidlaw Industries, 2 boys 2 girls.

Half Way to the Moon (1948, Mills & Boon). The Brown Fields (Mills & Boon). Dangerous Intruder (Mills & Boon). Young Bar (Mills & Boon). A Day Like Spring (Mills & Boon). Bridge of Corvie (Mills & Boon). Dear Tom (Mills & Boon). A Secret to Tell (Mills & Boon). April (Collins). A Family Affair (Mills & Boon). A Long Way from Home (Mills & Boon). The Keepers House (Mills & Boon). On My Own (Collins). Sleeping Tiger (Collins). Another View (Collins). The End of the Summer (Collins). Snow in April (Collins). The Empty House (Collins). The Day of the Storm (Collins). Under Gemini (1976, St Martins Press USA). Mills & Boon books published under pseudonym Jane Fraser.

Plays: The Dashing White Sergeant (with Charles Campbell Gairdner). The Piper of Orde. The Tulip Major.

Over Pilmore, Invergowrie, by Dundee. Longforgan 239.

Quigley. John
Born Glasgow. Feature writer with Beaverbrook Newspapers until 1962. Left to write novels and export Scocth whisky. Commercialised Clanrana, an old Scottish liqueur.

To Remember with Tears (1963, Hutchinson). The Bitter Lollipop (1964, Hutchinson). The Secret Soldier (1966, Hutchinson). The Golden Stream (1970, Collins). The Last Checkpoint (1972, Collins). King's Royal (1975, Hamish Hamilton).

Killearn, Stirlingshire.

Rae, Hugh Crauford
Born Glasgow 1935. Educ. Knightswood School, Glasgow. Married, one daughter. Bookseller's assistant to 1964: professional novelist, 1964-75. President of the Scottish Association of Writers.

Skinner (1964, Blond). Nightpillow (Blond). The Interview (Blond). A Few Small Bones (Blond). The Saturday Epic (Blond). The Marksman (Constable). The Shooting

Gallery (Constable). The Rock Harvest (Constable). The Rookery (Constable). Harkfast (1976, Constable). Writing as *Robert Crawford:* The Shroud Society (Constable). Cockleburr (Constable). Kiss the Boss Goodbye (Constable). Whip Hand (Constable). The Badger's Daughter (Constable). Two for the Grave (Robert Hale). And other pseudonymous novels.

Several TV and one radio play.

Drumore Farm Cottage, Balfron Station, Stirlingshire. 21-50-274.

Reid, Alexander
Born 1914. Trained as journalist. Has been editor of the *Scots Review* and *Saltire Review.*

Two Scots Plays (Collins). Steps to a Viewpoint—Poems (Dakers). Zoo-Illogical Hymns (Hutchinson). The Young Traveller in France (Phoenix Press). Paris (Phoenix Press). *Plays:* Worlds Without End. The Lass wi' the Muckle Mou. The Warld's Wonder. Diana. The Wax Doll. Voyage Ashore.

35 Craiglea Drive, Edinburgh 10.

Riddell, Alan
Born Australia 1927. Educ. Sydney; Merchiston Castle School, Edinburgh; Edinburgh Univ. Has worked as a journalist in Edinburgh, London, Melbourne, Sydney, Athens. Has been a sub-editor on the *Daily Telegraph* for past 13 years. Editor of the Scottish poetry magazine *Lines* 1952-55 and 1961-67.

Beneath the Summer (1953, Macdonald). Majorcan Interlude (1960, Macdonald). Edit. Scottish Section, Young Commonwealth Poets (1965, Hutchinson). The Stopped Landscape (1968, Hutchinson), awarded Scottish Arts Council Poetry Prize. Eclipse (1972, Calder & Boyars). Edit. Typewriter Art (1975, London Magazine Editions). Since 1963 his creative work has been almost exclusively in the field of concrete and visual poetry. In addition to exhibiting his own work in many countries he has organised two exhibitions in Britain and is at present organising the first international exhibition of photopoetry for the Central London Polytechnic in 1977.

23 Chapel Side, London W2. 01-727 0221.

Ritchie, J. T. R.
Born Edinburgh 1908. Along with N. McIsaac and R. Townsend founded Norton Park Group. Scripted four 16mm films. Happy Week End, The Singing Street, The Grey Metropols and The Flower and the Straw.

The Singing Street (1951, Albyn Press). The Singing Street (1964, Oliver & Boyd). Golden City (1965, Oliver & Boyd). Cinema of Days (1966, Albyn Press).

Plays: Something Valuable Going Cheap (1970, Lunch Hour Theatre, Edinburgh). Feature programmes and plays, Scottish radio, 1940s and 1950s. Stories and talks, Scottish radio, 1950s and 1960s.

16 Cairnmuir Road, Edinburgh EH12 6LP. 031-334 1865.

Ritchie-Calder, Lord, Baron of Balmashannar
Born Forfar. Educ. Forfar Academy, Edinburgh Univ. Reporter on *Dundee Courier*, 1922-24, *Sunday Post*, 1924-26, *Daily News*, 1926-29, *Daily Chronicle*, 1930. Pioneered science reporting *Daily Herald*, 1931-41. Director of Plans and Operations, Foreign Office, 1941-45. Special Adviser Supreme Headquarters 1945. Science Editor, *News Chronicle*, 1945-57. Editorial Board, *New Statesman* 1945-58. Professor of International Relations, Edinburgh University, 1961-67. Life Peerage 1966. Consultant and head of missions for United Nations. Kalinga Prize for promotion of the common understanding of science. Victor Gollancz Award for services to humanity. WHO Medical Science Medal. Member of Council, British Assoc. Exec. Chairman, UK Metrication Board.

Birth of the Future (1934, Barker). Conquest of Suffering (1935, Methuen). Roving Commission (1935, Methuen). Lesson of London (1941, Secker & Warburg). Carry on London (1941, EUP). Start Planning (1941, Kegan Paul). Man Against the Desert

(1951, Allen & Unwin). Profile of Science (1951, Allen & Unwin). The Lamp is Lit 1951, WHO). Men Against Ignorance (1953, UNESCO). Man Against the Jungle (1954, Allen & Unwin). Science in our Lives (1954, Mentor, USA). Science Makes Sense (1955, Allen & Unwin). Men Against the Frozen North (1957, Allen & Unwin). Magic to Medicine (1958, Aldus). Medicine and Man (1958, Allen & Unwin). Ten Steps Forward (1958, WHO). The Hand of Life (1959, Weidenfeld). The Inheritors (1960, Hutchinson). Agony of the Congo (1961, Gollancz). The Life Savers (1961, Hutchinson/Pan). Common Sense about a Starving World (1962, Gollancz). Living with the Atom (1962, Chicago Univ. Press). World of Opportunity (1963, United Nations Pubs.). Two Ways Passage (1964, Heinemann). Evolution of the Machine (1968, American Heritage). Man and the Cosmos (1968, Pall Mall). Leonardo and the Age of the Eye (1970, Heinemann). How Long Have We Got? (1972, McGill-Queens Univ. Press). Pollution of the Mediterranean (1972, Herbert Lang). Contri. to Encyclo. Britannica. Numerous programmes on radio and TV.

1 Randolph Place, Edinburgh. 031-225 5565.

Ross, Ian Anthony
Born Beauly, Inverness-shire 1917. Educ. Inverness Royal Academy, Edinburgh Univ., Dominican Order. Received into Roman Catholic Church, 1937. Entered Dominican Order, 1939. Ordained priest, 1945. Post graduate work in Scottish history at Edinburgh Univ., 1947-50. Nine years work in England. University Chaplaincies (R.C.) Edinburgh and Heriot-Watt. Chairman Scottish Catholic Historical Assoc. Some time director *Scottish International Review*. Chairman Edinburgh Cyrenian Trust.

Edit. Gude and Godlie Ballatis (1940, Oliver & Boyd). Contri. to Scottish Verse, 1851-1951 (1952, Nelson). The Golden Man (1955, Blackfriars Pubs.). Early Scottish Libraries, with John Durkan (1961, Burns, Glasgow). Contri. to Essays on the Scottish Reformation 1513-1625 (1962, Burns, Glasgow). Contri. to Whither Scotland? (1971, Gollancz). Scottish Blackfriars in the 17th Century (1972, Burns, Glasgow). Contri. to John Knox, New Assessments series (1976, Ramsay Head Press). Historical, religious and social work programmes for TV and radio.

25 George Square, Edinburgh EH8 9LD. 031-667 2287.

Royle, Trevor
Born Mysore, India, 1945. Educ. Madras Coll., St Andrews; Aberdeen Univ. Editor, William Blackwood, 1968-70. Literature Director, Scottish Arts Council since 1971. Guest editor, Pembroke Magazine, University of North Carolina, 1976.

We'll Support You Evermore, with Ian Archer (1976, Souvenir Press). Edit., with Edwin Morgan and Philip Ziegler, Scottish Short Stories 1976 (1976, Collins).

6 James Street, Edinburgh 15. 031-669 2116.

Saunders, R. Crombie
Born 1914. Edited *Scottish Arts and Letters*, 1944-48; *Scottish Angler*, 1948-53; *Scots Independent*, 1953-54.

XXI Poems (1953, Macdonald). The Year's Green Edge (1955).

Scott, Alexander
Born Aberdeen 1920. Educ. Aberdeen Academy, Aberdeen Univ. Served in Royal Artillery 1941-43, commissioned 1943, transferred to Gordon Highlanders, 1943, wounded in Normandy, 1944, awarded Military Cross at the Reichswald Forest, 1945. Married Catherine Goodall, 1944; two sons. Editor, *North-East Review*, 1945-46. Asst. lecturer in English, University of Edinburgh, 1947. Lecturer in Scottish Literature, University of Glasgow, 1948; senior lecturer, 1963; head of Department of Scottish Literature, 1971. Co-editor, *Scots Review*, 1950-51; editor, *Saltire Review*, 1954-57. General editor, The Scottish Library (Calder & Boyars), 1968-71. General editor, The Scottish Series (Routledge), 1971-75. General editor, The Makars Series (Scotsoun, Glasgow), 1974- . General editor, Scottish Books (Carcanet Press, Manchester), 1975- . Member of editorial board, *The Scottish Review*, 1975- . Sec., Universities Committee on Scottish Literature, 1968- . Member of Council and of Editorial Board;

Assoc. for Scottish Literary Studies, 1970-74; sec., 1974-76; pres., 1976. Member of Council, Scottish Text Soc., 1971- . Member of Council, Lallans Soc., 1972-74, pres., 1974- . Member of The British Council, 1972- . Member of the Literature Comm., Scottish Arts Council, 1975- .

Verse and Drama: Prometheus 48 (1948, S.R.C., Aberdeen). The Latest in Elegies (1949, Caledonian Press, Glasgow). Selected Poems (1950, Oliver & Boyd). Untrue Thomas (1952, Caledonian Press). Mouth Music (1954, Macdonald). Cantrips (1968, Akros). Greek Fire (1971, Akros). Double Agent (1972, Akros). Selected Poems 1943-1974 (1975, Akros). A Double Scotch with Edwin Morgan (1974, Claddagh Records, Dublin).

Prose: Still Life: William Soutar (1958, Chambers). The MacDiarmid Makars 1923-1972 (1972, Akros). Modern Scottish Literature 1920-1975 (1976, Carcanet Press).

Edited: Selected Poems of William Jeffrey (1951, Serif Books). The Poems of Alexander Scott (1952, Oliver & Boyd). William Soutar, Diaries of a Dying Man (1954, Chambers). Ten Medieval Makars (1975, Scotsoun). William Soutar, Poems (1976, Scotsoun). Sydney Goodsir Smith, Under the Eildon Tree (1976, Scotsoun). *Co-edited:* Contemporary Scottish Verse 1959-1969 (1970, Calder & Boyars). The Hugh MacDiarmid Anthology (1972, Routledge). Neil M. Gunn: The Man and the Writer (1973, Blackwood). Scottish Poetry 7 (1974, Univ. of Glasgow Press). Scottish Poetry 8 (1975, Carcanet). Scottish Poetry 9 (1976, Carcanet).

Plays: Right Royal (1954, Citizens' Theatre, Glasgow). Tam o Shanter's Tryst (1955, Citizens' Theatre, Glasgow). Truth to Tell (1958, Citizens' Theatre, Glasgow).

TV and radio: Seaman's Sang, broadcast 1947. The Volcano, broadcast 1948. Sodger frae the War Returns, broadcast 1949. Uneasy Lies, broadcast 1950. Cutty Sark, broadcast 1951. The Jerusalem Farers, broadcast 1951, published as Killer Crusade in *Akros* 1971. Untrue Thomas, broadcast 1952. The Deil's Awa, broadcast 1953. Shetland Yarn, in *New Plays Quarterly* 1954. Right Royal, broadcast, 1956, televised 1958. Truth to Tell, broadcast 1956. The Last Time I Saw Paris, verse play, *Saltire Review* 1957. The Monsters, broadcast 1962. Charles Murray (1864-1941), broadcast 1964. Heart of Stone, televised 1966, 1967, broadcast 1968. A Scart for St Andrew, broadcast 1975.

5 Doune Gardens, Glasgow G20 6DJ. 041-946 1844.

Scott, Paul Henderson
Born Edinburgh 1920. Educ. Royal High School, Edinburgh; Edinburgh Univ. Army 1941-47. Diplomatic Service, 1947- .

Bolivia (1956, HMSO). Contributor to *Twentieth Century, Economist, Blackwood's,* etc.

40 House O' Hill Road, Edinburgh 4. 031-332 3484.

Scott, Tom
Born Glasgow 1918. Educ. Thornwood School; Hyndland Secondary; Madras Coll., St Andrews Univ.; Edinburgh Univ. Left school at 14, worked as builder's labourer-apprentice, clerk etc. War service England and Nigeria. Ten years in London; Edinburgh since 1953. Atlantic Award in Literature 1950. Married Heather Fretwell; 1 son, 2 daughters. Life-long interest in singing, has sung professionally (bass). Sees literature and politics as head and tail of same coil. Scot. nat.

Seeven Poems o Maister Francis Villon (1952, Pound Press). An Ode til New Jerusalem (1965, Macdonald). The Ship and Ither Poems (1963, Oxford). Dunbar: An Exposition of the Poems (1966, Oliver & Boyd). Oxford Book of Scottish Verse, co-ed. John MacQueen (1966, OUP). Late Medieval Scots Poetry (1967, Heinemann). At the Shrine o the Unkent Sodger (1958, Akros). Tales of King Robert Bruce (1969, Pergamon; 1975, Reprographia). Penguin Book of Scottish Verse (1970, Penguin). True Thomas, with Heather Fretwell (1971, Oxford). Brand the Builder (1975, Ember Press).

In many poetry anthologies. Has several books still to be published including two vol. history of Scottish literature and critique of Robert Fergusson. Poems broadcast by BBC Home Service and Radio 3.

3 Duddingston Park, Edinburgh.

Sharp, Alan
A Green Tree in Gedde (1965, Joseph). The Wind Shifts (1967). The Hired Man (1971). Now writing film scripts in America.

Shepherd, John Alfred
Born Edinburgh 1913. Educ. George Watson's Coll., Edinburgh; St Andrews Univ. FRCS Edinburgh, FRCS England. Surgeon Capt., RNR. Consultant surgeon, Liverpool. Lecturer in surgery, Liverpool Univ. Member of council, RCS Edinburgh.
Surgery of the Acute Abdomen (1960, Livingstone). Concise Surgery of the Acute Abdomen (1975, Livingstone). Spencer Wells (1965, Livingstone). Simpson and Syme of Edinburgh (1970, Livingstone).
The Paddock, Well Lane, Heswall, Merseyside. 051-342 2477.

Shepherd, Nan
Born Cults, Aberdeenshire, 1893. Educ. Aberdeen High School for Girls; Aberdeen Univ. Lecturer in English Literature at Aberdeen College of Education, 1915-56. Chairman, Aberdeen Branch, Saltire Soc.
Novels: The Quarry Wood (1928, Constable). The Weatherhouse (1930, Constable). A Pass in the Grampians (1933, Constable). *Poems:* In the Cairngorms (1934, Moray Press).
503 North Deeside Road, Cults, Aberdeen AB1 9ES. 0224-47373.

Simpson, Myrtle L.
Born 1931. Educ. 19 various schools. Father in Army, always on the move, though basically Edinburgh. Climbed in Scottish hills since 15, and led various expeditions: Scottish Andean Exp. 1957; Trans-Greenland Exp. 1965; British North Pole Exp. 1969, etc. Mungo Park Medal 1968. *Daily Telegraph* Medal 1968. Has been comm. member Scottish PEN. President Scottish Ski Club.
Home is a Tent (1964, Gollancz). White Horizons (1966, Gollancz). Due North (1968, Gollancz). Simpson the Obstetrician (1969). Greenland Summer (1972, Gollancz). Armadillo Stew (1974, Blackie). Umiak (1975, Blackie).
Numerous TV contributions *e.g.* Globetrotter, BBC 1975.
2 Kirklee Terrace, Glasgow. 041-339 25z9.

Skinner, Alisdair
Drama lecturer. Activities have included promoting professional theatre with the Scottish Arts Council.
Plays: The One-to-One (1971, Traverse, Edinburgh). The Man Who Liked Walking on Sofas (1972, Byre, St Andrews).

Smith, Iain Crichton
Born 1928. Educ. Nicolson Institute, Stornoway; Aberdeen Univ. Teacher in English in Oban High School.
The Long River (1955, Macdonald). Thistles and Roses (1961, Eyre & Spottiswoode). The Law and the Grace (1965, Eyre & Spottiswoode). Consider the Lilies (1968, Gollancz). The Last Summer (1969, Gollancz). From Bourgeois Land (1970, Gollancz). Selected Poems (1970, Gollancz). Love Poems and Elegies (1970, Gollancz). Survival without Error (1970, Gollancz). The Black and the Red (1973, Gollancz). Hamlet in Autumn (1972, Macdonald). Goodbye Mr Dixon (1974, Gollancz). The Notebooks of Robinson Crusoe (1975, Gollancz). The Village (1976, Club Leabhar).
Poems, short stories and plays in Gaelic.
42 Combie Street, Oban, Argyll.

Smith, Janet Adam
The French Background of Middle Scots Literature (1934, Oliver & Boyd). Barbara Napier (1936, Moray Press). Heroic Ventures (1937, Moray Press). While the Candles Burn (1951, Maclellan). The Secret Messenger (1957, Inter. Pub. Co.).

Plays: The Road to the Coast (1935, Palladium, Edinburgh). The Seneschal (1938, Dean Studio, Edinburgh). Piping on the Hill (1952, Byre Theatre, St Andrews). Tell the Bees (1954, Adam House, Edinburgh). Scripts for features, schools and Children's Hour, BBC.
Addistoun, Ratho, Newbridge, Midlothian.

Smout, Thomas Christopher
Born Birmingham 1933. Educ. Leys School, Cambridge; Clare Coll., Cambridge. Worked at Edinburgh University since 1959. Now Professor of Economic History. Married to Anne-Marie Schoning (Danish) 1959, one daughter, one son. Chairman, Barony Housing Association.
Scottish Trade on the Eve of Union, 1660-1707 (1963, Oliver & Boyd). A History of the Scottish People, 1560-1830 (1969, Collins; Fontana paperback, 1972).
19 South Gillsland Road, Edinburgh EH10 5DE. 031-447 1066.

Spark, Muriel
Born Edinburgh. Educ. James Gillespie's School for Girls, Edinburgh. General Sec. Poetry Soc. and editor *Poetry Review*, 1947-49. FRSL 1963; OBE 1967; Hon. D.Litt., Strathclyde, 1971.
Edit. Selected Poems of Emily Bronte (1952). Child of Light, a Reassessment of Mary Shelley (1951). John Masefield (1953). Edit. Bronte Letters (1954). The Fanfarlo and Other Verse (1952). Collected Poems I (1967).
Fiction: The Comforters (1957). Robinson (1958). The Go Away Bird (1958). Memento Mori (1959). The Ballad of Peckham Rye (1960). The Bachelors (1960). Voices at Play (1961). The Prime of Miss Jean Brodie (1961, play 1966, film 1968). Girls of Slender Means (1963). The Mandelbaum Gate (1965, James Tait Black Memorial Prize). Collected Stories I (1967). The Public Image (1968). The Driver's Seat (1970). Not to Disturb (1971). Hot House by the East River (1973). The Abbess of Crewe (1974, filmed 1976). The Takeover (1976). Published Macmillan.
c/o Macmillan & Co., Ltd., 4 Little Essex Street, London WC2.

Squair, Olive M.
Born London 1902. of Scottish parentage, with Gaelic-speaking relatives. A journalist all working life—newspaper reporter, theatre critic, book reviewer, woman's page editor, advertising, in Scotland and England, both on the staff of newspapers and as a freelance news-reporter for the national press. For over 50 years associated with movements for Scottish self government. When working in pre-war London, was a member of six Scottish societies, including the London Gaelic choir; played violin and joined in exhibition Scots dancing for charity. Held office in the Institute of Journalists, and later in the NUJ, acting as a delegate at the amalgamation negotiations of the two bodies. Member Scottish and International PEN. Fellow of Society of Antiquaries Scotland.
The Quest of Ailsa MacRae, with introduction by C. M. Grieve (Mascot Press). A Tale to Tell (1970, Club Leabhar). Scotland in Europe: a Study in Race Relations (1976, Graphis Publications, 3 volumes). Also short stories and children's stories.
5 Balvicar, by Oban, Argyll PA34 4TF.

Steel, Tom
Born Edinburgh 1943. Educ. Daniel Stewart's Coll., Emmanuel Coll., Oxford. Programme researcher, Rediffusion Television, 1965. Producer, Thames Television, 1968.
Life and Death of St Kilda (1975, Fontana).

Steven, Campbell R.
Born Helensburgh 1911. Educ. Merchiston Castle, Edinburgh; Queen's College, Oxford. In business; part-time writing until 1966. Thereafter full-time writer. War service 1939-45; Captain in Army Commandos. Church elder; work at St Ninian's Church of Scotland training centre, Crieff. Member of Scottish Mountaineering Club; former member Alpine Club.

119

The Island Hills (1955, Hurst & Blackett). Scotland: Panorama-Books Series (1964, Andermann Verlag, Munich). The Central Highlands: Scottish Mountaineering Club District Guide (1968, Scottish Mountaineering Trust). Glens and Straths of Scotland (1970, Hale). Enjoying Scotland: Foyle Travel Book Club choice (1971, Hale). Proud Record: the Story of the Glasgow Fire Service (1975, Glasgow Corporation). The Story of Scotland's Hills (1975, Hale).

Weedville, 22 Havelock Street, Helensburgh, Dunbartonshire G84 7HQ. 0436-2942.

Stewart, A. J. (as playwright, Ada F. Kay)

Born 1929. After service in the ATS became a professional playwright. On BBC Television as staffwriter-adaptor, 1957-59, thereafter returned to Scotland as freelance playwright and author. Vice-chairman, Scottish Soc. of Playwrights.

Falcon: the Autobiography of His Grace James IV, King of Scots (1970, Davies). *Stage plays:* Cardboard Castle (1951, Blackpool). Warp and Weft (1952, Blackpool). The Man from Thermopylae (1961, Gateway, Edinburgh). *Television plays:* Red Rose for Ransom (1958). No Through Line (1959). A Question of Time (1959). Song for a Sparrow (1960). Hills beyond the Smoke (1961). Also six-part adaptation of Charlotte Bronte's Villette (1957). *Radio plays:* Red Rose for Ransom (1956, BBC Prize Winning Play). The Man from Thermopylae (1956). Documentary: The Life of Elizabeth Gaskell (1956).

33 Howe Street, Edinburgh 3. 031-556 4028.

Stewart, Ena Lamont

Born Glasgow 1912. Educ. Woodside School, Glasgow; Esdaile College, Edinburgh. Trained Aberdeen Public Library (4 years). Secretarial training. Medical Secretary, Radcliffe, Lancs; on secretarial staff of Medical Superintendent, Royal Hospital for Sick Children, Glasgow. Married 1941 late TV and stage actor, Jack Stewart; Div. 1 son. Returned to library work as librarian of Baillie's Reference Library, Glasgow. Occasional lecturer (Further Education, Glasgow Univ.) on local history, bibliography, creative writing. Former comm. member Old Glasgow Club; former editor and council member Clan Lamont Soc.

Radio: Play, Gaudeamus Igitur. A number of short stories.

Plays: Distinguished Company (1943, Rutherglen). Starched Aprons (1946, Glasgow Unity Theatre; 1947, Rev. Glasgow and Little Theatre, Edinburgh; 1948, Embassy Theatre, London; 1953, Rev. Embassy). Men Should Weep (First production Athenaeum Theatre, Glasgow, by Unity Theatre. Subsequent productions Queens' Glasgow and Little Theatre, Edinburgh. Embassy Theatre, London. Toured. Revived in Season of Scots Plays by Unity, Theatre Royal, Glasgow, 1948. The Heir to Ardmally (1957, Pitlochry Festival Theatre). Business in Edinburgh (1971, Citizens' Theatre). Walkies Time (First directed by David Birch for Pitlochry's "Coffee Morning Try-out." Subsequent Scottish Society of Playwright's Workshop, Glasgow and Edinburgh directed by Martin Heller, 1974. Full production, Edinburgh Netherbow directed by Charles Bell, March, 1975). Towards Evening (Scottish Society of Playwright's Workshop directed by Martin Heller. Full production, Edinburgh Netherbow directed by James House, March, 1975).

50 Airlie Street, Glasgow G12 9SN. 041-334 3545.

Stewart, Mary

Born Sunderland 1916. Educ. Eden Hall, Penrith; Skellfield School, Ripon; Durham Univ. Lecturer in Eng. Lang. and Lit. Durham Univ 1941-45. Married (1945) Frederick Henry Stewart (Sir Frederick Stewart). Regius Professor of Geology, Edinburgh Univ. Chairman of Advisory Board of the Research Councils.

Madam, Will You Talk (1954). Wildfire at Midnight (1956). Thunder on the Right (1957). Nine Coaches Waiting (1958). My Brother Michael (1959). The Ivy Tree (1961). The Moon-Spinners (1962). This Rough Magic (1964). Airs Above the Ground (1965). The Gabriel Hounds (1967). The Wind Off the Small Isles (1968). The Crystal Cave (1970). The Hollow Hills (1973). Touch Not the Cat (1976). *For Children:* The Little Broomstick (1971). Ludo and the Star Horse (1974). All published by Hodder.

Radio plays: Lift from a Stranger (1957). Call Me at Ten-Thirty (1958). The Crime of Mr Merry (1958). The Lord of Langdale (1958).

c/o Hodder & Stoughton Ltd., St Paul's House, Wainside Lane, London EC4P 4AH.

Stirling, Jessica
Born and lives in Glasgow. Married, two daughters. Began writing short stories before turning to novels.

The Spoiled Earth (1973, Hodder). The Hiring Fair (1976, Hodder).

Stuart, Alice Vandockum
Born Rangoon 1899. Her father was managing proprietor of *The Rangoon Gazette*. Educ. St Hilda's School, Edinburgh; Somerville Coll., Oxford. English mistress in schools in England and Scotland, 1923-36. Teacher of English to foreign students, 1941-45. Tutor in English poetry, Edinburgh Coll. of Speech and Drama, 1945-48. Lilian Bowes Lyon Award of Poetry Soc., 1955. Vice-pres., Edinburgh Musical (Competition) Festival Assoc. Vice-chairman, Scottish Assoc. for Speaking of Verse. Hon. Member, Soc. of Teachers of Speech and Drama.

Poetry: The Far Calling (1944, Williams & Norgate). The Dark Tavern (1953, George Ronald). The Door Between (1963, Macpherson, Dunfermline). The Unquiet Tide (1971, Ramsay Head Press). *Prose:* David Gray, the Poet of the Luggie (1961, Burgh of Kirkintilloch). Edit., with Charles Graves, Voice and Verse, Jubilee Anthology of the Scottish Assoc. for Speaking of Verse (1974, Ramsay Head Press).

57 Newington Road, Edinburgh EH9 1QW. 031-667 4383.

Tait, Robert
Born 1943. Edited *Scottish International Review* 1968-73.

Poems by Alan Hayton, Stephen Mulrine, Colin Kirkwood and Robert Tait (1967).

Taylor, John Wilfred
Born Dundee 1909. Educ. St Andrews Univ. Married, three children. Interested in Aviation meteorology.

Scot Free (1953, Reinhardt). Scot Easy (1955, Reinhardt). Scotland in Colour (1973, Batsford).

14 Jordan Lane, Edinburgh EH10 4RA. 031-447 6116.

Thompson, Francis
Born Stornoway, Isle of Lewis. Educ. Nicolson Institute, Stornoway. Married, four children. Lectures in electrical engineering in Inverness Technical College. Founder-Director of Club Leabhar, the Highland Book Club.

Electrical Installation Technology (1968-1972 (3 vols.), Longman). Harris and Lewis (1968, David & Charles). Harris Tweed, the Story of an Island Industry (1969, David & Charles). St Kilda and Other Hebridean Outliers (1970, David & Charles). Ghosts, Spirits and Spectres of Scotland (1972, Impulse). The Highlands and Islands (1974, Hale). The Uists and Barra (1974, David & Charles). The Supernatural Highlands (1975, Hale). Victorian and Edwardian Highlands and Islands (1975, Batsford).

Contributor of talks and short stories to BBC Scottish Radio.

31 Braeside Park, Balloch, Inverness IV1 2HJ. Culloden Moor 689.

Thompson, Ruth D'Arcy
Born Broughty Ferry, Angus, 1902. Educ. Rothesay House, Edinburgh; St Leonards, St Andrews; R.C.M., London. Professional musician and teacher of singing. Organiser of New Concerts Ass., from 1946-50 and of Freemasons' Hall Recitals from 1951-62.

D'Arcy Wentworth Thompson, The Scholar-Naturalist (1958, OUP). The Remarkable Gamgees (1974, Ramsay Head Press).

18 Frederick Street, Edinburgh EH2 2BH. 031-225 2350.

Thomson, David Cleghorn
Born Edinburgh 1900. Educ. Edinburgh Academy; Edinburgh Univ.; Balliol Coll., Oxford.

Verse: Far and Few (1919, Blackwell). The Hidden Path (1932, Maclellan). I Would be Acolyte (1943, Oliver & Boyd). *Plays:* Five One-act Plays for a Scots Theatre (Oliver & Boyd).

Thomson, Derick Smith (Gaelic form, Ruaraidh MacThomais)
Born Stornoway 1921. Educ. Nicolson Institute, Stornoway; Univs. of Aberdeen, Cambridge and Bangor. Professor of Celtic, Univ. of Glasgow. Previously on staffs of Edinburgh and Aberdeen Univs. Ossian Prize (FVS Foundation, Hamburg), 1974. Chairman, Gaelic Books Council. Pres., Scottish Gaelic Texts Soc. Member Scottish Arts Council. Editor of *Gairm*, Gaelic quarterly, since 1952. Editor *Scottish Gaelic Studies*, 1961-76.

The Gaelic Sources of MacPherson's Ossian (1952, Oliver & Boyd). Branwen Verch Lyr (1961, Dublin Inst. for Advanced Studies). Edit., with Ian Grimble, The Future of the Highlands (1968, Routledge). Intro. to Gaelic Poetry (1974, Gollancz). The New Verse in Scottish Gaelic (1974, Univ. Coll., Dublin). Ceol na Gaidhlig: cassette and book (1975, Scotsoun). *Gaelic verse:* An Dealbh Briste (1951, Serif Books). Samradh is Foghar (1967, Gairm Pubs.). An Rathad Cian (1970, Gairm Pubs.). Special issue of *Lines* devoted to his verse (1971, Macdonald).

41 Aytoun Road, Glasgow G41 5HW. 041-423 7573.

Thomson, George Malcolm
Born Leith 1899. Educ. Daniel Stewart's Coll., Edinburgh; Edinburgh Univ. Married (1) Else Ellefsen (d. 1957) one son, one daughter; (2) Diana van C. Robertson.

Caledonia, or The Future of the Scots (1927, Kegan Paul). A Short History of Scotland (1930, Kegan Paul). The Twelve Days (1964, Hutchinson). The Crime of Mary Stuart (1967, Hutchinson). Sir Francis Drake (1972, Secker and Warburg). The North West Passage (1975, Secker and Warburg). Warrior Prince (1976, Secker and Warburg).

5 The Mount Square, London NW3 6SY. 01-435 8775.

Todd, Ruthven
Born 1914.

Poetry: Ten Poems (1940). Until Now (1942). Acreage of the Heart (1944). Planet in My Hand (1946). Mantelpiece of Shells (1954). Garland for the Winter Solstice (1961). *Prose:* Over the Mountain (1939). Lost Traveller (1943). Tracks in the Snow (1946). William Blake the Artist (1971).

Toulmin, David (John Reid)
Born Rathen, Aberdeenshire, 1913. Left school at fourteen to work on farms. Worked on the land for 44 years. Moved into Aberdeen and took up landscape gardening at 58. Still working and writing at 62. Ardent cinema-goer for 50 years. Has written published essays on the cinema.

Hard Shining Corn (1972, Impulse). Straw into Gold! Scots Miscellany of fact and fiction (1973, Impulse). Blown Seed: A Scottish novel (1976, Paul Harris).

Short stories broadcast on Radio 4. Seven volumes of manuscript diary: extracts in *The Leopard* magazine, Aberdeen.

7 Pittodrie Place, Aberdeen AB2 1QN.

Tranter, Nigel
Born Glasgow 1909. Educ. St James' Episcopal School and George Heriot's School, Edinburgh. RASC and RA, 1939-45. Trained as accountant. Pres. E. Lothian Liberal Assoc., 1960- . Pres. Scottish PEN, 1962-66. Chairman, Soc. of Authors, Scotland, 1966-72.
Fiction: Trespass (1937, Moray Press). Mammon's Daughter (1939, Ward Lock). Harsh Heritage (1940, Ward Lock). Eagle's Feathers (1941, Ward Lock). Watershed

(1941, Ward Lock). The Gilded Fleece (1942, Ward Lock). Delayed Action (1944, Ward Lock). Tinker's Pride (1945, Ward Lock). Man's Estate (1946, Ward Lock). Flight of Dutchmen (1947, Ward Lock). Island Twilight (1947, Ward Lock). Colours Flying (1948, Ward Lock). Root and Branch (1948, Ward Lock). The Chosen Course (1949, Ward Lock). Fair Game (1950, Ward Lock). High Spirits (1950, Collins). The Freebooters (1950, Ward Lock). Tidewrack (1951, Ward Lock). Fast and Loose (1951, Ward Lock). Bridal Path (1952, Ward Lock). Cheviot Chase (1952, Ward Lock). Ducks and Drakes (1953, Ward Lock). The Queen's Grace (1953, Ward Lock). Rum Week (1954, Ward Lock). The Night Riders (1954, Ward Lock). There Are Worse Jungles (1955, Ward Lock). Rio D'Oro (1955, Ward Lock). The Long Coffin (1956, Ward Lock). MacGregor's Gathering (1957, Hodder). The Enduring Flame (1957, Hodder). Balefire (1958, Hodder). The Stone (1958, Hodder). The Man Behind the Curtain (1959, Hodder). The Clansman (1959, Hodder). Spanish Galleon (1960, Hodder). The Flockmasters (1960, Hodder). Kettle of Fish (1961, Hodder). The Master of Gray (1961, Hodder). Gold for Prince Charlie (1962, Hodder). Drug on the Market (1962, Hodder). The Courtesan (1963, Hodder). Chain of Destiny (1964, Hodder). Past Master (1965, Hodder). A Stake in the Kingdom (1966, Hodder). Lion Let Loose (1967, Hodder). Cable from Kabul (1968, Hodder). Black Douglas (1968, Hodder). The Steps to the Empty Throne (1969, Hodder). The Path of the Hero King (1970, Hodder). The Price of the King's Peace (1971, Hodder). The Young Montrose (1972, Hodder). Montrose, Captain-General (1973, Hodder). The Wisest Fool (1974, Hodder). The Wallace (1975, Hodder). Lords of Misrule (1976, Hodder). *Non-Fiction:* The Fortalices and Early Mansions of Southern Scotland (1935, Moray Press). The Fortified House in Scotland Vol. 1 (1962), Vol. 2 (1963), Vol. 3 (1965), Vol. 4 (1966, Oliver & Boyd). Vol. 5 (1970, Chambers). Land of the Scots (1968, Hodder). The Queen's Scotland—The Heartland (1971, Hodder). The Queen's Scotland —The Eastern Counties (1972, Hodder). The Queen's Scotland—The North-East (1974, Hodder). The Queen's Scotland—Argyll & Bute (1976, Hodder). Portrait of the Border Country (1972, Hale).
Children's Novels: Spaniards' Isle (1958, Brockhampton Press). Border Riding (1959, Brockhampton Press). Nestor the Monster (1960, Brockhampton Press). Birds of a Feather (1961, Brockhampton Press). The Deer Poachers (1961, Blackie). Something Very Fishy (1962, Collins). Give a Dog a Bad Name (1963, Collins). Silver Island (1964, Nelson). Pursuit (1965, Collins). Fire and High Water (1967, Collins). Tinker Tess (1967, Dobson). To the Rescue (1968, Dobson).
Children's Non-Fiction: Outlaw of the Highlands—Rob Roy (1965, Dobson). Pegasus Book of Scotland (1964, Dobson).
Quarry House, Aberlady, East Lothian EH32 0QB. Aberlady 258.

Tremayne, Sydney (Durward)
Born Ayr 1912. Educ. Ayr Academy. Thirty-six years in Fleet Street. Formerly chief sub-editor of the *Daily Mirror* in London, later for 24 years leader writer of, first, the *Daily Mirror* and then the *Daily Herald.*
Verse: For Whom there is No Spring (1966, Pendulum). Time and the Wind (1948, Collins). The Hardest Freedom (1951, Collins). The Rock and the Bird (1955, Allen and Unwin). The Swans of Berwick (1962, Chatto and Windus). The Turning Sky (1969, Hart-Davis). Selected and New Poems (1973, Chatto and Windus). In many anthologies.
Blawan Orchard, Westerham Hill, Kent. Biggin Hill 729111.

Turner, William Price
Poet, novelist, playwright. Gregory Fellow in poetry, Leeds Univ., 1960. Writer in Residence, Glasgow Univ., 1973-75.
The Moral Rocking Horse (Barrie & Jenkins). Hot Pot (Constable).

Ure, Joan
Playwright and poet. Lives at Castle Douglas.
The Hard Case. I've Got one Friend (Scottish Theatre Edits).

123

Urquhart, Fred
Born Edinburgh 1912. Educ. Several village schools; Stranraer High School; Broughton Secondary School, Edinburgh. Worked in an Edinburgh bookshop; in a London literary agency. Reader for MGM (1951-54). Reader and editor for Cassell, publishers (1951-74) and various other London publishers. Occasional journalism. Book reviewer for *Time and Tide*, *Books of the Month*, *Sunday Telegraph*, *Oxford Mail* and *Times Educational Supplement*.

Time Will Knit (1938, Duckworth). I Fell for a Sailor (1940, Duckworth). The Clouds Are Big With Mercy (1946, Maclellan). Selected Stories (1946, Fridberg). The Last G.I. Bride Wore Tartan (1948, Serif). The Ferret Was Abraham's Daughter (1949, Methuen). The Year of the Short Corn (1949, Methuen). The Last Sister (1950, Methuen). Jezebel's Dust (1951, Methuen). The Laundry Girl and The Pole (1955, Arco). Edit. W.S.C. Cartoon Biography of Winston Churchill (1955, Cassell). Scottish Short Stories (1957, Faber). The Dying Stallion (1967, Hart-Davis). The Ploughing Match (1968, Hart-Davis).

Many stories broadcast by BBC. Stories have appeared in numerous anthologies. Won the Tom-Gallon Trust Award in 1951, and received Arts Council bursaries in 1966 and 1975.

Spring Garden Cottage, Fairwarp, Uckfield, Sussex. Nutley 2511.

Watson, Roderick
Born Aberdeen 1943. Educ. Aberdeen Grammar School; Aberdeen Univ.; Peterhouse, Cambridge. Ph.D. at Cambridge on poetry of Hugh MacDiarmid. Awarded Writer's Bursary from Scottish Arts Council, 1970-71. Currently lecturer in English at Stirling University. Co-editor of annual *Scottish Poetry* anthology for 1974 and 1975.

28 Poems (1964, Aberdeen Univ. Poetry Soc.). Parklands Poets No. 7 (1970, Akros). Trio (1971, New Rivers Press, New York). True History on the Walls (1976, Lines Review Editions). Hugh MacDiarmid (1976, Open Univ. Press).

Poems and short stories broadcast on BBC 4 and BBC 3 Radio.

19 Millar Place, Stirling FK8 1XD. Stirling 5971.

Watson, William
Born Edinburgh 1931. Educ. Edinburgh Academy; Merton Coll., Oxford. On staff of *The Scotsman*, 1954-73: variously tea-boy, Literary Editor, Features Editor, etc. Presently Literary Advisor, Perth Theatre, Perth.

Novel: Better Than One (1969, Barrie & Rockliff: Cresset Press). *Play:* Sawney Bean, with Robert Nye (Calder & Boyars).

Plays: Sawney Bean, with Robert Nye (1969, Traverse Theatre). A Footstool for God (1972, Pitlochry Festival Theatre). The Larch (1974, Perth Theatre). Dodwell's Last Trump (1975, Perth Theatre).

Edgelaw Farmhouse, Carrington, Midlothian. Temple 206.

Webster, David
Born Aberdeen 1928. Educ. Woolmanhill Coll. of Physical Educ. Winner of many sports awards and championships. Commonwealth Games Team Official. Olympic Technical Official. Formerly senior Technical Representative, Scottish Council of Physical Recreation and Head of Facilities Planning, Scottish Sports Council. Patron, Scottish Games Assoc. Chairman, Scottish Amateur Weightlifters Assoc. Director of Leisure and Recreation, Cunningham District Council.

Modern Strand Pulling (1954, G. Grose). Complete Physical Book (1963, Arlington). Defying Gravity (1964, A. Murray). Two Hands Snatch (1967, Radler, USA). Lifting Illustrated (1967, Duplicats). Scottish Highland Games (1973, Reprographia). The Iron Game (1976, D. P. Webster & IWF). Contributions to TV programmes.

43 West Road, Irvine, Ayrshire. Irvine 72257.

Weir, Molly
Born Glasgow. Educ. Hyde Park School; Skerry's College; Glasgow Univ. Named fastest shorthand writer in Britain. Studied drama and voice production, joined Pantheon Club and worked as freelance writer in Glasgow. Broadcast, film, stage and television actress.
Molly Weir's Recipes (1960, Collins). Shoes Were for Sunday (1970, Hutchinson). Best Foot Forward (1972, Hutchinson). A Toe on the Ladder (1973, Hutchinson). Stepping into the Spotlight (1975, Hutchinson). Radio scripts and weekly column in *People's Journal*.

Weir, Tom
Gave up Ordnance surveying in 1950 to climb in the Himalayas and begin professional photography. Specialising in photo-journalism and travel went on from there travelling and adventuring and writing about it. Hon. Vice-Pres. Scottish Rights of Way Society.
Highland Days (1948, Cassell). Camps and Climbs in Arctic Norway (1954, Cassell). Ultimate Mountains (1953, Cassell). East of Katmandu (1955, Oliver & Boyd). The Scottish Lochs Vol. 1 (1970, Constable). The Scottish Lochs Vol. 2 (1972, Constable). Western Highlands (1973, Batsford). Colour Book of Highlands (1975, Batsford). Scottish Islands (1976, David & Charles). The Highland Line (1974, Famedram). Scotland's Threatened Lines (1974, Famedram).
Broadcasting: Feature Programme, Weir's Way, 28 minutes. 8 programmes, Scottish Television. Roving Reports—Scotland Today. Scottish Television. Radio; Afield and Twelve Noon.
Gartocharn, Dunbartonshire. Gartocharn 260.

White, Kenneth
Born 1936.
Poetry: Wild Coal (1963). En Toute Candeur (1964). Cold Wind of Dawn (1966). The Most Difficult Area (1968). *Prose:* Letters from Gourgonnel (1966). Cosmos (1960). Travels in the Drifting Dawn (1972).

Williams, Gordon
Born Paisley 1934.
From Scenes Like These (1968, Secker & Warburg). The Camp (1967). The Upper Pleasure Garden (1970). Walk, Don't Walk (1972). Big Morning Blues (1974). Hazell Plays Solomon, with Terry Venables under pseud. of P. B. Yuill (1976, Penguin).

Wilson, Conrad
Born Edinburgh 1932. Educ. Daniel Stewart's Coll., Edinburgh. Music Critic of *The Scotsman* since 1963; previously sleeve-note editor for Philips Records in Holland and Music Critic of Edinburgh *Evening Dispatch*. Editor since 1966 of Edinburgh Festival opera and concert programme notes. Member Critics' Circle.
A Critic's Choice (of gramophone records) (1966, Corgi Books). Scottish Opera: The First Ten Years (1972, Collins). Collins Encyclopedia of Music (Revised Edition, 1976, Collins). Donald Francis Tovey (1977, Ramsay Head Press).
29 India Street, Edinburgh EH3. 031-226 2859.

Wilson, Norman
Born Edinburgh. Formerly director John Menzies, Edinburgh; managing director, Wyman Marshall, London. Served with Ministry of Information during the War. Founder of Edinburgh Film Guild. Chairman, Edinburgh Film Festival, 1947-59. Former member of Council, Edinburgh International Festival. Founder member, Films of Scotland. Former Governor, British Film Institute. Edited *Cinema Quarterly*, *Film Forum*. Founded Ramsay Head Press, 1971. Vice-chairman, Scottish General Publishers Assoc. OBE.
Projecting Scotland (1945, Film Guild). Edit. Scotland and the Scots (1974, Ramsay Head Press). Scottish Writing and Writers (1977, Ramsay Head Press).
72 Great King Street, Edinburgh EH3 6QU. 031-556 4534.

Wither, Jack
Born Glasgow 1935. Educ.—"destroyed by war and illness." Became apprentice motor mechanic and electrician. National service—"learning to hate." Wandered Europe. Became youth worker, unsuccessful. Started writing. Now works in Goethe Institute Library.
Plays: The Sleeping Giant (1971, Cumbernauld Cottage Theatre). Radio Plays: The Sleeping Giant, A Perfect Arc, Islands, and shorter pieces. TV Plays: Hard Sell, Two in a Box (BBC Scotland).
247 West Princes Street, Glasgow.

Wright, Allen
Born Edinburgh 1932. Educ. George Watson's College, Edinburgh. Arts editor and drama critic of *The Scotsman* since 1965.
J. M. Barrie: Glamour of Twilight (1976, Ramsay Head Press). Reviews and features for radio and many publications.
Inglewood, 286 Gilmerton Road, Edinburgh. 031-664 1554.

Wright, Ronald Selby, the Very Rev.
Born 1908. Educ. Edinburgh Academy; Melville Coll.; Edinburgh Univ. Minister of the Canongate (Kirk of Holyroodhouse) and Edinburgh Castle since 1937. Army chaplain during the War. Moderator of the General Assembly, Church of Scotland, 1972-73. CVO, DD, FRSE. Chaplain to the Queen.
Asking Them Questions (1, 1936; 2, 1938; 3, 1950, OUP). Asking Them Questions, New Series (1, 1972; 2, 1973, OUP). Fathers of the Kirk (1960, OUP). Asking Why (1939, OUP). Soldiers Also Asked (1943, OUP). Take Up God's Armour (1969, OUP). The Kirk in the Canongate (1956, Oliver & Boyd).
As the Radio Padre broadcast for many years.
Manse of the Canongate, Edinburgh EH8 8BR. 031-556 3515, Farend, 5 Tantallon Terrace, North Berwick. 0620-6415.

Wright, Tom
Born Glasgow 1923. Worked in etched and stained glass and mural painting for some years. Taught art in schools. Army 1942-47. Graduated at Strathclyde Univ., where he held a fellowship for some time. Currently script adviser to drama dept., BBC Scotland.
Plays: The Mask, The Comeback, Pygmies in the Colosseum, There Was a Man, Sir Walter Was, And They'r a' Deid. *Radio Plays:* The Mask, Ane Stick of Brume, Markheim, The End of the Game, Jack in a Box. *Television Plays:* The Comeback, Darkness on Duncan, There was a Man, The End of the Game, Jack in a Box, Can I Speak to Col Barnes?, Tactical Foul, Stobo Takes the Chair, Initiative Test, Portrait of My Love, The Bloodletting. *TV Series:* This Man Craig, The Borderers, Cargo Maquire, Sutherland's Law, Poet's Places, Garnock Way, Between the Lines.
Poetry: Interim Report (1959, New Orleans Poetry Journal). Completed Stevenson's Weir of Hermiston (1975, Holmes McDougall). Many TV adaptations, short stories, film scripts.

Wyatt, Stephen
Lecturer in Drama at Glasgow Univ. Has directed many plays.
Plays: Take Diogenes (1973, Little Theatre, London). Exit Pursued by a Bear (1973, Edinburgh Festival).

Wynd, Oswald
Born Tokyo, of Scots missionary parents. Educ. Glasgow Univ. Served with Intelligence Corps in Malaya. Spent three and a half years as prisoner of war in Japan where he began his novel Black Fountain, which gained the Doubleday Award in 1947.
Black Fountains. When the Ape is King. Stubborn Flower. Moon of the Tiger. Summer Can't Last. The Devil Came on Sunday. Walk in the Long Dark Night.
Also writes thrillers under the name of Gavin Black.

Young, Douglas
Educ. Aberdeen Univ. Taught in Univ. of Victoria, BC, before becoming lecturer in English at Aberdeen Coll. of Education.
Beyond the Sunset: A Study of James Leslie Mitchell (Lewis Grassic Gibbon) (1973, Impulse).

Youngson, Alexander John
Born 1918. Educ. Aberdeen Grammar School, Aberdeen Univ. Professor of Political Economy at Edinburgh Univ., 1963-74. Director, Research School of Social Sciences, Australian National Univ., 1974- .
The American Economy, 1860-1940 (1951). Possibilities of Economic Progress (1959). The British Economy, 1920-57 (1960). The Making of Classical Edinburgh (1966). Overhead Capital (1967). After the Forty-five (1973). Beyond the Highland Line (1974).